As an army daughter, Philippa Annett lived in fourteen houses in eight countries before she was sixteen. Bound tightly to her family as they travelled the world, schooled initially by her mother and then at military forces' schools, her inspiration to write was developed early by all that she experienced along the way.

Philippa comes from a family of chroniclers and her belief in the value of family stories provides the rich foundations for *Heavy Luggage*, as it did for her debut novel, *The Diamond Fund*.

Philippa and her husband live in Somerset. They have three children and eight grandchildren.

In loving memory of Mark and our parents

Philippa Annett

HEAVY LUGGAGE

Philippa Annett

With contributions from
Mark Hilpern

AUSTIN MACAULEY PUBLISHERS™
LONDON · CAMBRIDGE · NEW YORK · SHARJAH

A CIP catalogue record for this title is available from the British Library.

ISBN 9781035846078 (Paperback)
ISBN 9781035846085 (ePub e-book)

www.austinmacauley.com

First Published 2024
Austin Macauley Publishers Ltd®
1 Canada Square
Canary Wharf
London
E14 5AA

I am hugely indebted to my brother, Mark, for his courageous and poignant contributions to our childhood story. And to my mother, for her initial help with detail. And to my family and friends, whose continued interest, enthusiasm and encouragement helped me finish *Heavy Luggage* when the going got tough. Thank you.

My brother, Mark, and I felt part of a mini tribe, separated as we saw it from the rest of the world by our exciting and easily romanticised childhood. With our dynamic father leading us to far flung military posts and our beautiful strong mother at the helm, we were a closed and loving unit, but not perfect. Together we decided to write down memories of our childhood as children of the British Army in the 1950s and 60s.

Introduction

<u>Mark</u>

I haven't ever really given much thought as to why people feel moved to write their memoirs. I suspect there may be many reasons from self-aggrandizement, narcissism or catharsis. I think I will go down the cathartic road. Also because my sister, Philippa, is undertaking this project and it is a fine way to sharpen one's pencil, the past being the past however you recall it. And I would find such indescribable pleasure in stumbling across an account of my parent's, grandparent's, great-grandparent's, or however far back of even a brief account of their lives. I believe it should be enshrined in law that such documents are attached to one's Will with a reduction in death duties with compliance! (I also believe that every house should have such a logbook!). So yawn you relatives as you wade your way through some of the detritus of our time on this earth. There are those from your loins and wombs who may find it of some interest down the line, so guard it well and make account of your own!

I was born in 1953, Philippa in 1950. We have lived very different lives, disagreed with each other on many subjects, however are very close. Perhaps as a result of this differential, my sister's memory is much sharper than mine and appears to start to emerge when she was circa three years old, whereas mine edges its way through the fog of time at circa five or six.

Our early historic childhood is punctuated by Geography. Which country comes next, waiting for the Heavy Luggage to arrive so we could surround ourselves with familiarity that was enough for us to call it home wherever or however long it may be. I / we felt part of a mini tribe and as long as we looked out for each other, no harm would befall us.

This theory was put through some serious test drives involving my mother in a near fatal car crash in Aden, my aunt's Fiat 500 bursting into flames with us in it, being shot at in Lebanon, an often contentious relationship between my parents, beautiful weekends on desert beaches with squiffy parents and their friends, and constant layers of chamomile cream that dried like pink chalk as post sun care in some of the hottest places on the globe.

For the most part, my sister and I could run free. We were fed and watered and loved, and I'm sure we gave out as much love as we got. But I doubt my parents weighed the balance. We were united against the rest of the world and felt invincible.

The Beginning

<u>Philippa</u>

Mark and I wake in the night to the sound of gunfire outside. I am seven years old. Mark is five. We are bleary and confused from sleep and have no time to feel afraid before our parents hurry into our bedroom. Our mother is tying a silk dressing around her waist. It's her Chinese one with the embossed dragon on its back. Father has shed his pyjamas and is struggling to do up his army combat trousers with one hand. In the other, he carries a paraffin lamp. On his upper body he wears a string vest, a garment in whose merits he has great confidence. His mouth is set grimly and he looks very angry. His expression inspires us with confidence, however. We have no doubt that he can 'sort things out'. Mother is calm, her movements are measured and her words offer comfort. This reassures us. We are too young to recognise that the way she is behaving reveals her fear. She normally moves and speaks very quickly. She lies down with us on the bed that is placed against the wall under the window and we wait. Father extinguishes the lamp and crouches like a panther beside us. The open window, with its mosquito-netting casement, allows us to hear male voices speaking outside, hushed and urgent. Then another volley of shots and bullets spray the side of the house. There is a soft thud against the wall above the bed on the opposite side of the room, where a few minutes earlier my brother had been sleeping. At the same time, a loud metallic

twang outside is followed by the frightened bray of a donkey.
Our donkey, Little Stick. Mother gasps.

"Bloody idiots," says Father. He springs up and marches
out of the room to sort things out.

A childhood memory is a curious thing. Because it's so
personal, it must inevitably be flawed. But it can, in whatever
state of truth, remain so immediate in our minds that the
interim might have stood still and the telling of it becomes the
present. This was one such event. One among many it has to
be said, in an event filled childhood.

My father was an officer in the British Army and, in those
days, the families followed the drum and accompanied the
soldiers to every posting. My father, mother, brother and I
were lucky enough to live in some of the most exotic and
exciting places on the army map and our experiences were
many and varied.

This time, we were in our home in Shemlan, a small
village high in the hills above Beirut in the Lebanon. It was
June 1958. Twelve months earlier, Father had been sent to
learn Arabic at MECAS (the Middle Eastern College of Arab
Studies, run by the Foreign Office) in Shemlan. The school
had been set up after WW2 by the British Government in
order to teach the Arabic language and culture to forces
personnel and diplomats. My mother always referred to it as
the 'Spy School', no doubt because the double Soviet Agent
George Blake had studied there. Ironically, Kim Philby,
another spy, attended MECAS to learn Arabic a few years
after my father. But perhaps better to start from the beginning
of it all.

Our parents met after the Second World War when they both started working for the Baata Shoe Company in Tilbury, East London. Before the war, Baata had built a vast factory and utopian township for the workers on what had been wasteland in the area, and the company had become a great economic success. The town contained hostels and houses for the hundreds of employees, as well as hotels for visitors, entertainment venues, shops, schools and even its own newspaper, the Baata Chronicle.

Our father had been a young subaltern during the war, his twenty-first birthday spent on the beaches of Normandy in the thick of battle. By the end of the war he had thankfully survived intact, although his recurring nightmares were doubtless evidence of the mental anguish he must have felt but kept to himself until he was much, much older. After being de-mobbed, he joined Baata as a salesman.

Our mother had trained as a press photographer with the Manchester Evening News in the war years, one of the first women in the country to take on such a job and made possible no doubt by the fact that many of the younger men who normally filled that role were away fighting in the war. Although slight, Mother was a strongly opinionated young woman and she was tough. She had to be. She carried her heavy equipment around to jobs, developed her photos in the newspaper's darkroom to meet deadlines and had no qualms about working in the male dominated environment. Inevitably, once the men returned from war, they wanted their jobs back so she was forced to leave. She decided to move south to London where her twin sister, Billie, was at art school and she joined the Baata Chronicle as a press photographer.

As unmarried employees of Baata both our parents, like the many other young people in the workforce, were housed in hostels, men and women segregated with many rules in place to make sure there was no nightly fraternising! With men back from the war, and women now finding a new independence, there was a strong sense of camaraderie and a vibrant social scene and I think our parents had a great deal of fun.

Mother and Father duly got engaged and a wedding date was set for April 23rd 1949. However, with strict moral codes in place, they were too impatient to wait and decided to get married sooner in secret. They booked a registry office on Tilbury Docks for the occasion and it was arranged that Mother's twin sister, Billie, and Father's best friend from army days, John Fincham, should be witnesses. (A quarter of a century later, after a failed marriage and many disastrous relationships, Billie married John, but that is a story for another time).

On the allotted January day however, there was a thick freezing fog. Trains were delayed and Billie and John were going to be late. Arriving at Tilbury Docks, our parents did the only thing they could and asked two dockers to act as witnesses to their marriage. The dockers agreed willingly and duly signed their names on the Marriage Certificate. Mr Grissle and Mr Rumble!

Mother and Father's secret marriage remained such and they went through a formal white wedding ceremony some months later, Mother wearing the same dress as both her sisters did for their weddings in the same church in Boden, Cheshire.

Soon after their marriage, Father's mother died and left them a bit of money with which they bought a house in Hampton Wick, complete with 'sitting tenants' in residence! The property had been cheap to buy for this reason but our parents were content to live on the first floor and lower basement. It was damp and dark and it was here, in December 1950, that I was born.

Eighteen months later, Father decided that 'civi-street' wasn't for him and he took the one momentous decision that formed my childhood and our future lives as a family. He re-joined the British Army.

Our Parents 'formal' Wedding—April 1949

Germany (1952 – 1954)

<u>Philippa</u>

Our first posting was to Germany in 1952. I was not quite two years old. My parent's house was sold and Father was immediately sent out to Germany. Post-war Germany was divided into zones, each one under the jurisdiction of Russian, American or British troops. The British had the area around the Rhine and it was here, in Dusseldorf, that my father joined his new regiment, the 19th Field Royal Artillery.

'Your father always manages to find a reason to get out of the packing,' Mother remarked more than once during my childhood. And it would appear to be true as he preceded us to every posting and, on what was to be their first taste of army life abroad, Father set this precedent by going on ahead! As luck would have it, Mother was a thoroughly independent woman who had no qualms about packing up and following the drum unaccompanied.

She and I duly travelled to Germany by rail from Waterloo, where the designated trains used by the army were assigned colours according to their destination. Military police were on hand to guide the army families onto the correct trains and the correct carriage. And as the wife of a junior officer, Mother was shown into a second class carriage for the journey to Germany, her first experience of the rigid class system in the army that dominated our lives from then on!

British forces families abroad lived a protected and somewhat cocooned lifestyle around the military bases, able to buy English food at the NAAFI (Navy, Army & Airforce Institution) and to take advantage of the free schools, libraries and medical care provided. And from the moment they arrived in a new posting, wherever they were in the world, there was an instantly supportive social circle in which everyone had a part to play. Much later, when I was a teenager and my father had finally left the army, we felt very isolated without the back-up of the greater military family around us.

Back then, on arrival in a new posting, married soldiers were allocated a house, or 'quarter', and the size of the house bore direct relation to the rank of the soldier. But it was also possible for the officers and their families to apply for a 'Hiring', which were local houses rented by the army. Arriving in Germany on that first posting, my parents were initially given a quarter, but setting a pattern they followed for most of their army life abroad, they applied for a Hiring and ended up in a large requisitioned German house in a leafy street in Dusseldorf.

In June 1953, my brother was born and our parents employed a young German Au Pair, Faylie, who lives only vaguely in the back of my memory. My mother also bought a Dachshund puppy called Fritzie who unfortunately grew up to develop the embarrassing habit of enthusiastically riding the legs of anyone who stood still long enough for him to get a grip, so he was re-homed to a farm! I don't remember Fritzie at all but I hope his new owners neutered him so that he could live a less stressful life and experience things other than the frustrating urges of his hormones!

We were in Dusseldorf for two years before Father's regiment was posted to Korea to join the Commonwealth ground forces fighting with the Americans in the Korean War. My mother, brother and I were sent back to the UK, the military police once again on hand to help with the journey. Once past Waterloo however, the army ceased to be responsible for us and we travelled on to Cheshire unaccompanied to be near my mother's family.

Our maternal grandmother lived in a large regency house in Bowdon, and although she was away working in Austria as a courier at the time, she had let the ground floor of her house to tenants and we were able to move into the self-contained upstairs flat. We lived here for the best part of a year, a longer time than our mother had expected. At the end of his regiment's time in Korea, Father had stayed on as a liaison officer with the American forces for a time. But when he finally left Korea to rejoin his regiment, who were then stationed in Hong Kong, we too were duly given our orders. Mother was sent a first-class ticket on the P & O Liner 'Chusan' and was expected to answer the call of the drum.

Having had no communication from Father for some time, Mother was unsure of what was waiting for her at the other side of the world, or what was expected of her. But she packed up our suitcases and, in October 1955, she, my brother and I set sail from Tilbury for the four week voyage to join Father in Hong Kong. I was five years old, my brother was three, and our mother was twenty-eight. The day before we left, our mother's aunt gave her £50 in cash.

"Sew this into your underwear," she told Mother. "You're expected to tip a lot in first class."

Introductions

**Family portrait before Father
left for Korea**

Hong Kong (1955-57)

Philippa

P&O Chusan

What I remember of that first sea voyage is more than likely confused with our voyage back from Hong Kong two years later on the *'Asturias'*, or the one out to Aden from the UK in 1959 on the *'Nevassa'*, for I was very young. But my collective 'snap-shot' recollections of life on board ship as a child form the backdrop to an evocative memory bank. The muffled throbbing of the ship's engines: the wonderful rocking horse in the first class nursery where my brother and I were obliged to play when the adults ate their meals; the smell of wood and paint and hot tar; the striped deck chairs on the wooden decks; the bow waves heaving and frothing away from the sides of the ship; and wild storms when the ship would heave and toss and huge waves break onto the windows of our cabin on the upper deck.

We stand on the deck of the 'Chusan' in Tilbury looking down at the crowds of people on the quayside below. They look up at us, a sea of pale faces and waving hands. As the huge ropes tying the ship are released and the tugs begin to push and pull the ship away from the quay, banners and streamers fly across the increasing gap, and I cover my ears as the ships horn blasts out its deep base notes in farewell.

Our first stop is Gibraltar and after the many quiet days at sea, during which we have settled into the routine on board ship, voices are now raised and orders given out as the ship docks. The gangplank is lowered and passengers depart and embark in a brief bustle of activity, a pattern that becomes habitual at every port we visit over the following weeks. Sometimes however, we merely drop anchor off shore and smaller vessels pull up alongside to deliver supplies or pick up mail. Mother has befriended two other army officer's wives and their children, also travelling out to Hong Kong to join their husbands, and we stand together along the landward deck railings watching the supply boats coming and going below us. The younger children are seated in their pushchairs, whilst we older ones lean against our mothers' full-skirted dresses.

We continue on through the Mediterranean and the weather becomes warmer. At Port Said, the entrance to the Suez Canal, dozens of little boats surround the ship, each one selling souvenirs, trinkets and local produce. The boats jostle violently against each other but the Arab traders keep their balance as they shout up to the passengers on the decks high above them, each clamouring to be heard above the other. And with a combination of calls, whistles and hand movements to indicate the desired item and charge, the passengers and traders begin the noisy process of haggling for an agreed price. Once bargains have been made, baskets on long ropes are lowered over the sides of the ship to collect purchases and deliver payment.

For us children, who sit cross-legged in a semi-circle on the floor of the saloon, the 'Gully Gully Man' comes on board to entertain us with his magic tricks. He wears white Egyptian robes with a red fez on his head, a pillbox hat topped with a black tassel. From under this hat, and accompanied by a patter of learnt English words, 'Chicken in my hat! Chicken in my neck!' he produces a seemingly endless supply of newly hatched yellow chicks.

'Gully Gully, Gully,' he says, grinning toothlessly. We are enthralled.

We ease into the Suez Canal, passing the huge statue of Ferdinand de Lesseps high up on its concrete plinth (this was destroyed the following year during the Suez Crisis by the Egyptian resistance) and a pilot launch approaches the ship. Mother tells us the pilot must come on board to guide us through the narrow channel. The ship's engines take on a new note then, quieter and more contained, and there's an air of expectancy on board. Everyone is up on deck watching the land beside them slip away and they talk in hushed tones. I peer through the thickly painted railings at a group of white robed Arabs who stand and watch us pass, their faces impassive. The flat characterless desert on either side is very close. Then the land falls away and the ship heaves too to allow the pilot to leave.

Now, we're out into the Red Sea and the shoreline becomes a more distant thin green strip against the dusty brown mountains fringing the horizons. The heat intensifies and we are glad of the small pool on board ship. We sail out into the Arabian Gulf and on through the Indian Ocean, where dolphins cavort alongside the ship and flying fish land on the deck. The ship's crew entertain the passengers by dropping lines of meat to attract the sharks, who turn as they came up to seize the bait, exposing the vicious curve of their teeth and the pale undersides of their bodies which gleam briefly beneath the churning water.

The outside world touches us for a short time when we dock; Aden, Bombay, Colombo, Penang and Singapore. When the gangplank is lowered from the ship to the quayside, Mother takes us with her to spend the day exploring whilst the ship takes on more supplies. These interludes are all too brief before the ship departs once more, but they provide unique but, sadly for me, only briefly remembered glimpses into communities and countries now lost.

When we reach Hong Kong, the mood on board ship changes. After four weeks at sea, and a somewhat lethargic cocooned isolation, all is now bustling expectancy. Packed suitcases and trunks are collected by the stewards and stowed along the corridors, cabin doors slam and people gather on deck. The engine noise diminishes as the ship slows to meet the tugs at the mouth of Kowloon harbour and we are guided slowly through a myriad of smaller vessels that crowd the *waters; wooden fishing boats known as Junks and the smaller flat bottomed Sampans, packed ferries sitting alarmingly low in the water, and vast cargo ships. It seems extraordinary that none of these vessels collide. We look to the land. A mix of white colonial and tall modern buildings line the shore and dark forested mountains rise up high behind them.*

As the Chusan slowly approaches the quay where we are due to dock, we see there is a crowd waiting behind a rope barricade. At first, they are a blurred mass of indistinguishable faces, most of them shielded by hats. But as the gap between the sides of the ship and the quay narrows, we passengers standing high up on the deck are able to look down and begin to search for friends or relations. The people around us shout and wave when they see who they are looking for and, one by one, the people on the quay join in, calling up words that are lost in the din. All at once everyone seems to be laughing or crying. The ship's ropes are slung across the receding gap to the waiting dockers on the quayside who loop them deftly around vast bollards, and the 'Chusan' gives a long final blast of her horn. Mother begins to wave frantically and call out our father's name.

'David. David!'

I see him then. He is wearing a white shirt and shorts and is very tanned after his stint in Korea. But there's too much noise and he doesn't hear. He continues walking towards the other end of the quay. Then the gangplank is lowered and Mother grabs our hands as we join the queue to leave the ship. I feel suddenly rather shy—it's been a while since we last saw him.

Mark

My earliest memories are possibly of our sea voyages. I certainly recall the excitement of departure, the smell of the freshly holy-stoned decks, and the first gentle movement of this, from my perspective, massive ship as she headed out to sea. On one occasion, a military band played *Sussex by the Sea* as we did so. I believe this would have been when leaving Hong Kong some years later when we had the Royal Sussex Regiment with us.

I have been drawn to the sea for much of my life and, possibly over-romanticising these first voyages, sometimes wonder if a seed was sown back then. Everything was exciting from running around on deck, sneaking under the tarpaulins into life boats, then Suez and the Gully Gully Man my sister describes. I have wondered from time to time if this funny little man in a fez may be a nascent reason that I've always been enthralled by magic, both as an art form and existentially.

Arriving in Hong Kong after that first voyage to a father one hardly knew, and things get hazier. I remember getting excited by the Junks and Sampans and the Stat Ferries, and the fish market and myriads of smells and noises. But almost all my other memories from Hong Kong are hidden beneath the stain of an accident I had which resulted in my small body suffering from serious burns.

I remember the pain, I think. I remember an out of body experience wrapped in a sheet in my mother's arms and looking down on the two of us. This is real. I made a complete recovery in due course as a result of first-class and, for then, cutting edge medical care.

Philippa

We come from a family of photographic chroniclers. My mother's father put together albums of photographs chronicling their lives in Hungary and Europe when she and her sisters were growing up. My father's mother was also a keen amateur photographer and her albums provide pictorial evidence of their life in East Africa when he was a boy. Both collections provide extraordinary snap-shots of a bygone age and of lost worlds between the wars.

Later, when we too travelled around the world with the army, and throughout our childhood, our mother always had a camera around her neck and took photographs of us and of the places in which we found ourselves. And I know that their many albums chronicling our life when we were growing up not only gave my brother and me all the pleasure of memories, but also provide a glimpse for us, and our children, into a world similarly much changed. Perhaps that's the real value of photograph albums. They help us remember who we are and where we fit into the context of global history as well as providing a vital pictorial family tree.

As an adult, I too have taken photographs throughout my life and created albums, all of which are much enjoyed by my family. I have as many albums as I have adult years, something which creates a great storage problem in my household, but although I now store my newer photographs on my computer, there is nothing quite like turning the pages of an old photo album and wondering at those images of the past, caught and chronicled forever onto shiny paper.

I turn the pages of the Honk Kong album now and feel such familiar tugs of recollection. I've grown up looking at these photographs admittedly, but I can nevertheless remember many of them being taken. There are sounds and smells involved in the memories so I don't doubt them. But most especially, I'm struck by how privileged our parents were to live in Hong Kong for two years and to see it as it was then. And I shall always feel enormously grateful to have this visual record to help me remember.

Before losing myself to memory forty plus years on however, I was drawn to learning a little more about Honk Kong and its history and to find out what the British Army was doing there in 1955.

I discovered that Britain first occupied the island of Hong Kong in the early 19th century, primarily as a military staging post in what became known as the Opium Wars between Britain and China. China's capitulation in 1841 resulted in Britain gaining Hong Kong as part of the subsequent initial peace treaty, the Treaty of Nanking, although the war and acts of aggression between the two nations continued throughout the second half of the 19th century. But by 1898, China had finally accepted defeat and agreed to sign Hong Kong over to the British on a ninety-nine year lease, this time giving Britain control not only of Hong Kong Island, but also of the many other islands around it and part of the mainland adjacent to it, which became known as the 'New Territories'. This agreement was dependent on Britain giving Hong Kong back to the Chinese at the end of the ninety-nine years.

As a British Colony, Hong Kong rapidly became a flourishing East-West trading centre, a position it enjoyed until the Second World War when, in December 1941, the colony was attacked and fell to the Japanese Army. The

Japanese then occupied Hong Kong for three years, during which the Chinese inhabitants were brutally treated and systematically executed. By the time it was liberated in 1945, by joint British and Chinese troops, the population had shrunk and the people remaining were starving and disease ridden.

In 1955 however, when we were posted to Hong Kong, the colony was beginning a period of unprecedented growth. The huge influx of refugees fleeing the 1949 Communist revolution in Mainland China had boosted the population and introduced a surge of cheap labour, capital and expertise and, despite the resulting severe housing problem, Hong Kong's industry, manufacturing and commerce enterprises were taking off. The British Army was responsible for the security and protection of the colony, and different units and regiments each spent time in Hong Kong for periods of up to three years.

Our father's regiment had been posted out to Hong Kong to do their stint whilst he was in Korea, and having rejoined it, Father was offered the opportunity to study for his staff college exams, the passing of which would guarantee him gaining a higher rank in his army career. Mother was always fairly disparaging of his efforts however, and told me he wouldn't 'knuckle down' to put in the necessary work and that he spent more than his fair share of time in the officers' mess instead of studying! He never attained a higher rank than major so I presume his results didn't pass muster. Father was such an active man, full of energy and enthusiasm for life, always looking for the next adventure, and I imagine there were just too many distractions for him at the time. I remember him sitting in our garden in Hong Kong, painstakingly producing a rather nice drawing of our home that always hung in my mother's house and now in mine, and it was certainly worth drawing, for by then we lived in a castle!

Our first home had been a flat in Lau Gardens in the mountainous Western part of the New Territories, from where my parents began to get to know their new surroundings. They bought a car and the foothills and mountains that rose up from the coast offered umpteen opportunities for exploring, walking and exploring being something my family excelled in wherever we were in the world! The highest mountain was Castle Peak, on whose granite slopes the ancient Tsing Shan Buddhist monastery and temple drew my adventurous parents like a magnet. We went up there on Christmas Day 1955 and Mother photographed Mark and me, each clutching what I imagine to be one of our favourite presents, with the view down the coast to Kowloon and across the bay to Hong Kong Island behind us. They drove miles inland, stopping for Mother to take photographs of the people and places they came across; of workers in paddy fields pulling rice and loading it onto carts being hauled by oxen, and ancient mud walled towns where the gates were still closed at night. And after a drive to the top of the New Territories, she photographed the view over to Mainland China, the words 'forbidden territory' bringing an echo of my parent's excitement to my memory of the occasion.

By the spring of 1956 however, and true to my parent's intention to try and avoid living in Army quarters, my father had found us a magnificent castellated folly in which to live. Castle Peak Lodge sat on the hillside just above Kadoori Beach, with spectacular views up to Castle Peak and out across the bay. The house was built from two types of stone, with deep covered verandahs underneath and turrets on top, all of which gave it a fairytale appearance. The downstairs windows were faced with decorative wrought iron, presumably to protect the house from theft. But it's the gardens I remember most clearly. They were beautifully mainucured, with ornamental trees at one end and a crazy paving pathway that wound its way around the edges of the lawns, past intermittent stone benches placed at strategic viewing points, and on through trees laden with scented flowers. One of them was a lychee tree whose clusters of heavy fruit was a joyful discovery for us all. I have adored lychees ever since! The pathway made a perfect track for Mark and me to pedal our tricycles around. For our first Christmas in Hong Kong, our parents had bought us one each. Mine was red and my brother's blue. They had a stepping platform on the back so that we could give each other rides.

There was a swimming pool to one side of the house but it was full of dirty water and weeds so we never used it. Behind the house were the kitchens, and beyond them a small stone house in which the gardener, Fah Wong, and his family lived. Fah Wong came with the house and lives on in our family's memory as the man who taught my mother to catch a snake with a forked stick. I vaguely remember the occasion, although I'm not sure my mother ever needed to put this skill into practice. But taking protection against vermin of one type or another was something we accepted as the norm.

Our beds were shrouded with mosquito netting and the legs of the beds placed in pots of oil to prevent scorpions and ants from climbing up. Having a bath meant looking out for the cockroaches that would regularly crawl out from the bath overflows and swim around in the bathwater. And we were never very far from a rat. My father had to kill one in the house once and we tried to block our ears against the noise of its screams as he did so.

The higher we climbed up the pine dotted hillside behind our house, with the heat bouncing off the dry stony slopes and the smell of vegetation strong as we disturbed the earth, the greater the view. We could look down onto Castle Peak Lodge with its circular turrets gleaming in the sun, and out beyond the beach to the sparkling waters of Kadoori Bay scattered with Junks, the wind filling their blood red sails.

There were wild cats living in these hills, and when one hid her kittens in the corner of our verandah, Father decided he'd try to get one of them for my mother. As he approached the litter, the mother cat flew at him and savaged his hand and arm before leaving and taking the kittens with her. This resulted in Father having to have a series of injections against rabies.

"Lilax," the Chinese doctor would tell him, before plunging the needle into his stomach. Father, however, would find it difficult to 'lilax'. He would tense the muscles in his stomach when the needle went in and, as he was very strong, broke many a needle in the process.

"Lilax," the doctor would repeat patiently, as he took another syringe and prepared to try again.

Mother got Mini soon after that, a tortoiseshell cat who had belonged to another army family leaving Hong Kong. Mini was very affectionate and loved to be carried around. But she was also rather fat and our cook would weigh her up and down in her hand as if to assess whether she was ready to eat.

"She plenty heavy, Missee, she plenty heavy!"

"No, no, no, Ah Ling!" Mother would say, grabbing Mini back from the Chinese woman's firm grasp. "Mini is not for eating!"

Mini survived our posting intact and was inherited by another family when we left.

Ah Ling was our first cook, 'very highly trained' according to Mother. But she produced such excellent meals that after one particular dinner party given by our parents at Castle Peak Lodge, the Canadian wife of a fellow Army officer sent her Amah (maid) around to call on Ah Ling to offer her twice the money Mother was paying her. Ah Ling and her assistant, Ah Fong, left immediately, leaving Mother with no help until Ah Oi and Mei Ghi arrived.

These two young women had both grown up at the Christian orphanage. Ah Oi was quite stern and had the scars of small pox on her face. Mei Ghi had a round smiley face and long plaits and could play Greensleeves on the recorder. I remember them both very fondly for, amongst other things, teaching Mark and me the Chinese equivalent of Conkers, a game played by taking two of the long thick pine needles that dropped from the trees, hooking them through each other and pulling to see which one breaks first.

Among the many other army families living in Hong Kong, our parents had a busy expat social life and Mark and I were never short of playmates. Mother's photographs capture us all swimming in the warm seas off Kadoori Beach and making sandcastles in the sand. There were also boat trips in junks, picnics in the hills and children's parties at Castle Peak Lodge. Our parents organised an Easter egg hunt for all the children in our garden, and on looking up at the hillside behind the house I was convinced that I saw the Easter Rabbit bounding amongst the boulders and wild flowers on his Easter egg mission. I became quite a celebrity for a number of years amongst other children when I told them what I'd seen. I suppose it could be argued that such is the unreliability of childhood memories! But some can never be other than what they were.

Castle Peak Lodge

San Pan Village

On Kadoori Beach

It's hair wash night and the bath is running. Ah Oi and Mei Ghi are helping Mother and there is much laughter and chatter as Mark and I take off our clothes and wait for the temperature of the water to be just right before we can climb in. It's a bit complicated as the taps are in different places. The cold water comes out of the tap at the end of the bath, but the hot water comes out of a large circular water tank that sits on a wooden board suspended over the bath. The water from that is boiling and we are always careful not to let any part of our body touch the tank or it burns us. Mei Ghi is in charge of the hot tap today and now she turns it off and says the bath is ready for us. Mark goes in first and lies down to get his hair wet. He squeals with pleasure, kicking out with his legs, and his foot knocks against the wooden plank. The tank of boiling water is sufficiently heavy for this not normally to be a problem, but no one has noticed that today one of its feet isn't sitting squarely on the board, and now the foot suddenly slips off. The boiling water inside lurches to one side and spills over the rim of the tank, sending a scorching torrent cascading down onto Mark. Somebody screams.

Mark was in hospital for several weeks with second-degree burns to his chest, left arm and hand. The doctor who treated him had gained practice on burns victims in the war, when it was observed that sailors suffering from burns who were rescued from the sea healed a lot quicker than those who weren't. Mark was, therefore, given daily salt baths, and after all the skin on his chest and arm had peeled away he slowly began to heal.

Mother wasn't allowed to stay with him in hospital, although he was only four, which must have been torture for her. But she went to be with him every day, driving down to Kowloon and across to Hong Kong Island on the car ferry to sit by his side. Mark took comfort in a Chinese rag doll he called Jimmy, from which he was inseparable. But Jimmy became so saturated by the copious amounts of fluid that seeped from Mark's wounds each night, that Mother had to replace him every day. Mark never knew.

Down on the coast below the house, Castle Peak Village is where we go to buy fish. We hold tightly onto Mother's hands as she surveys that day's catch; dead fishes bloodily displayed in baskets and live lobsters and crabs, their claws tied together, defenceless against the boiling water that would later end their lives. The Chinese vendors crouch on the ground beside them, their faces inscrutable. The smell of fish is overpowering. The women are dressed in tunics and loose trousers and the men in white tee shirts, their trousers rolled up. They all wear round straw hats with pointy tops. They are tiny, golden skinned, graceful people. Our mother fits in somehow. She is small with high cheekbones, dark hair and is deeply tanned by the sun.

At the edge of the village, Chinese families live on the beach in small covered sanpans pulled up onto the sands. From here the men catch their fish in huge triangular nets that they sling out into the sea from the water's edge. The women carry their babies on their backs, tied on with a shawl. Lines of flapping washing hang between the boats and the shore. And on some of the boats, dogs are tied up to await an unthinkable fate. When my mother looks down into the view finder at the top of her Rolleiflex camera, groups of children stop what they are doing to stand, thin and naked, to watch us watching them.

We leave Hong Kong in October 1957, sailing back to England on the Troop Ship 'Asturias' on what is to be her last voyage. I am nearly seven, and Mark is four and a half. We arrive in Southampton four weeks later to begin a month's leave in the UK before our posting to the Lebanon. The 'Asturius' is then famously used in the making of the film *A Night To Remember* about the Titanic, before being stripped and broken up.

HMT Asturias

Our mother wrote about this voyage…

'After all the weeks of packing and preparations it's almost a relief when the time actually comes to board ship and leave.

Almost! The final goodbyes were sad, and saddest of all was to leave such a lovely, lovely place, our home for nearly three years, and so many memories.

'This is an old German ship captured during the war and converted into a troopship. She now has the requisite blue line of a troopship around her hull and around her two funnels. She's a bit of an old tub, but there is an old-fashioned grandeur about her. She came from Korea before picking us up in Hong Kong and is carrying the Royal Sussex Regiment bound for Gibraltar, where their families will join them. They've done their years' stint of fighting in Korea and will no doubt be glad to see their wives again. Apart from David and me, there are only a few other married families on board, but we will pick up a few more at Singapore. Before that we have a weeks' long voyage through the China Sea in which to settle into the routine of life on board and to get to know one another.

'Our cabin is dark with a lot of heavy wood furnishings but is fairly large with two sets of bunks and we all four fit quite neatly one on top of the other. We have two windows that look out onto B deck and it's heavenly to lie in bed and watch the blue sea go by. The only hazard is if anyone should pass by on the deck and peer in! But this doesn't often happen since the deck is supposed to be for the families only and there aren't many of us.

'We arrive in Singapore, which is amazing, but as always time is too short to see as much as we'd like. We visit the obvious places like Raffles, etc. and it's good to be riding in a rickshaw again. Odd when I remember how embarrassed I was about that when we first got to Hong Kong! But now it seems so natural and I love it.

'The regiment on board carry their own band, so we not only get a band playing ashore to welcome the ship as she docks and sails, but we also have our own music en route. Rather nice, and they have a very nifty dance band too which plays each evening after dinner. Officers and families only in our section mind you! The troops have their own quarters and mess decks and one sees very little of them.

"Strange to know there are so many of them. I ask the executive officer if I could go and see where they lived, but he said that it wouldn't be on since they'd been without women for a year and he couldn't vouch for their reaction to 'an attractive young woman' amongst them! I wonder what he thinks they'd do! However, he did say that that the officers would be arranging a dance or two for the troops and that we, the ladies, would be expected to attend. A foot bruising operation he said it would be, but I for one look forward to it.

'The new families are settling in. We now have a total of nine children on board, and some of the wives have organised part-time schooling and other things for them. Good old army wives put their hands to most things! Philippa and Mark are having a whale of a time.

'The weather becomes hot and sticky and the sea rather rough. We are told we're on the edge of a typhoon.

'We are now well used to washing ourselves and our clothes in sea-water, and have been given special bars of soap designed for the purpose. Not very satisfying as they don't bubble up, but better than going dirty. But the clothes are taking on a distinctly stiff look and feel. There is a ships' laundry thank goodness that tackles uniforms and more complicated things, which is just as well, for ironing is jolly hot and, in this rough weather, no picnic. All the ship's bathing and laundry facilities are inboard, in the middle of the vessel, and although they have a sort of primitive air conditioning it gets unbearably hot in there.

'The couples who came on board at Singapore are proving very good value, and our evenings have become much more jolly. There are now rehearsals for a concert, to be performed on the night before we get to Gibralter. It should be a hoot as some of the chaps are even dressing in drag and have been scrounging the odd garment from us all!

'We dock at Colombo in Ceylon and a group of us go to swim on a wonderful beach below Mount Lavinia. I've never seen such a beach! A huge sweep of bay, fringed with golden sands and palm trees. Quite lovely. I'd love to visit Ceylon again one day. It's very Raj. Tea plantations in lovely mountains and the people seem nice.

'It's good to put out to sea again however. One gets used to always being on the move. The weather is getting even hotter now but the sea much calmer as we cross the Indian Ocean. We watch flying fish, dolphins and sharks.

'Aden is our next stop and what a disgusting place this is! I stand on deck with the children and stare at the oil refineries all around and there's a dreadful smell of oil in the air. The place is colourless, barren and rocky, with mountains inland shrouded in a pink haze. The main town of Steamer Point has an air of colonial grandeur I suppose, but it's a matter of comparisons, an oasis in a desert, and I've never felt such heat! Even the Arabs seem lethargic, crouching or standing around on street corners, staring at us visitors as though we had come from a different planet. Seen from the sea on leaving, there is an uninhabited stillness about the coastline, very mysterious and rather inviting. But I am not sorry to leave. The weather remains unbearably hot, even at sea, and we can't seem to get rid of the smell of the place. Even the water tastes of oil, and when I complained about this, I was told that we were obliged to take on water there since bunkering had been difficult in Ceylon, hence the taste!

'We enter the Suez Canal at night after taking on a pilot at Suez. Whilst the children sleep, some of us adults stay up to watch and are mesmerised by the full moon, the bright clear stars and the endless desert all around.

'Port Said is, as always, remarkable, with Gully Gully men (much to the children's delight), bum-boats and all. I want to buy a pouffe and a wooden camel train and a backgammon set but I gather we're not docking there or going ashore, so it has to be done over the side of the ship. My purchases are stowed with the heavy baggage somewhere below decks along with all those troops, a world apart.

'The ship's concert is a great success and we've already been to two troop's dances. As predicted, very hard on the feet but well worthwhile. A nice bunch of men, and some not here of their own free will, many being national service soldiers.

'The Mediterranean is such a different experience. You wouldn't think that endless sea could be so different, but it is. We dock at Gibraltar and the ship feels very empty when the men have all gone.

'Next stop, Southampton.'

Leave

Grandma's House in Boden, Cheshire

Philippa

We never had a permanent home in England, so our visits to the UK in between our postings involved us in a whirlwind of much-anticipated and mildly celebratory visits to family. We would pile into whichever car our parents were driving and our first port of call was usually to see Mother's twin sister, Billie, who lived in Richmond with her husband, Jack.

Billie was glamorous in a completely different way to Mother. She was a very accomplished artist and both she and Jack worked at J Walter Thompson, an advertising company at the forefront of modernity. Billie and her friends were independent, childless, career women who wore bright colours and smoked heavily, and as such seemed rather alien, their lifestyle so very different from our mother's and the other army wives we knew.

Leaving them, we would drive up to Cheshire where our mother's older sister, Joan, her husband, John, and their family lived, as well as their mother, our Grandma, and other assorted relations. We then would head back down to Henley on Thames to visit our paternal grandfather and his wife, maybe seeing Father's two sisters and our other cousins at the same time.

Occasionally, we drove on down to Polperro in Cornwall to visit our father's aunt and his cousins. And at every destination, there were family parties, picnics, walks or pub lunches to mark our visit.

In Cheshire, Joan's two sons, our cousins, were the same age as Mark and me and we had a lot of fun together throughout our childhood, at each visit managing to pick up our relationships seamlessly from where we had left off two years previously. Later, Joan and John had a third child, a daughter called Margaret Anne (named after Joan's favourite doll as a child), or Miggit for short.

When I was younger, I found it hard not to question whether they thought it boring to have lived in the same house all their lives. How supercilious that must have sounded to them. But I believe it came from a place of puzzlement rather than an awareness of our privaledged life. They would assure me that they left their home once or twice a year to go on holiday, usually to Wales, where they owned a converted railway carriage in a field. This sounded a lot of fun, although the concept of 'holidays' remained lost on me at that time.

But whilst I could never imagine living in the same house forever, the homes of our grandparents were a comforting constant to me. Grandma's house in Bowden had been home to our mother and her two sisters from their teenage years. It was here that they finished their growing up, dated their first boyfriends and left to pursue their careers, Billie and Joan to art school and Mother to the Manchester Evening News, and later from where they all got married.

When the girls left home, Grandma worked in Europe for a few years and turned the ground floor and upper floor temporarily into two self-contained apartments, the upstairs one of which we lived in when Father was in Korea. On her return, she lived in the ground floor rooms and continued to let the upstairs flat. When Grandma grew old, her living quarters shrank further when she had her bed moved into the back breakfast room, which was always warm. The other downstairs rooms were left to guests. Eventually, when old age and loneliness became too hard to bear, she chose to sell her house and move into a rather gracious home for the elderly where I believe she was content. But that was much later, after I had grown up.

Despite all its changes, for me as a child Grandma's house had a continuity about it that consolidated its status as 'home'. It held stories behind the floor to ceiling sash windows, echoes of welcomes and farewells on the covered terrace, and of family reunions and celebrations spilling from the gracious sitting room out onto the long laurel fringed lawns. I remember the house as being full of laughter, especially if my mother's two sisters were with us too. With their shared sense of the ridiculous and an innate ability to get completely lost in glorious silliness, it was as if they and Grandma shed all pretence of adulthood when they were together and their joy was wonderfully contagious.

At the back of the house, the breakfast room with a little kitchen and bathroom attached was where Grandma cooked stews for lunch and boiled eggs for tea and, on Sundays, turned the wireless up high for the morning Service and sang along loudly with the hymns in a wavy voice. She knew every word. Beyond the kitchen was a yard with a coal-shoot down to the cellars and a door out onto a back alleyway. There was also an outside loo where spiders lived and the paper was always Bronco. Here, on one visit, I fed a stray cat for some days without Grandma knowing (she didn't like cats). Mother and I walked in secret up the road to the village shop where I stood on a stool in order to see over the high wooden counter and ask for cat food.

Grandma was small and round and seeped in the evocative scents of 4711 and Fox's Glacier mints. The latter, transparent sweets individually wrapped in twists of blue paper, were kept in a glass container on her bureau, from where they would be offered if we were lucky but given reluctantly if we asked! In the top drawer of her bureau was a pair of magnet dogs, one white and one black, with which Grandma would enthusiastically entertain us when we were young. She had a natural exuberance and lack of inhibition that was often at odds with what was otherwise, in those days, a fairly strict code of expected behaviour, and as a result she was more than often frowned upon by our father!

Our mother and her two sisters were born in Budapest where their father worked for an English manufacturing company. They lived a privileged life in a moderately grand house with servants and a governess, a prerequisite number of social obligations and regular European travel.

But at the start of World War Two, our grandmother and the three girls were forced to flee by train, returning to Cheshire to Grandma's large extended family. Mother and Billie were eleven and Joan just eighteen months older.

Our grandfather stayed behind and, in what still remains a rather mysterious guise, worked undercover throughout the war helping, amongst other things, Jewish children escape Nazi Europe. One such boy, whose family were sent to the concentration camps and killed, ended up living with Grandma and the girls in England for some years. In the meantime, Grandfather fell in love with a Czechoslovakian woman who worked with him and, after the war, he came home and asked my grandmother for a divorce.

Grandma was left very well provided for and it was then that she purchased the house in Bowden where she continued to bring the girls up as best she could. But rejection, and what was in those days the huge stigma of divorce, left its mark on her emotional health, and the three girls became a closed unit in their protection of her. Possibly because of this, or arguably the impact of their father's withdrawal from them, all three suffered with issues of insecurity in their adult lives. Our mother thankfully proved to be the strongest of the three, but both her sisters went on to struggle with depression and alcohol dependency and died tragically in middle age as a result. But that was much later. When I was young, all I remember was the laughter and fun they all had together and rejoice in that.

Our father's family had no less an eventful past. His father, our Granddad, lived with his wife, who we called Granny Betty, and a Boxer dog called Tusker (who only lives in my memory on account of his tendency to bowl us over and then to slobber over us) in a brick and flint-stone cottage in the middle of the countryside high up in the hills outside Henley on Thames. Pond Cottage was so called after the large pond in the front garden. During the winter the pond iced over and we would slide about on it whilst holding onto Father's hands.

The front garden had a rickety wooden gate leading out into the fields where, in the summer, cows grazed under huge sweeping oak trees. It was in these fields, with Granddad in his cord trousers, baggy tweed jacket and huge boots and us holding onto his rough warm hands, that we had our first introduction to the British countryside. He showed us how to rub dock leaves over stinging nettle rash, he showed us the acorns lying on the ground like little eggs in cups, he showed us how to find and eat blackberries and, by default, we learnt that cow pats may look crispy on the outside but on the inside they weren't!

Inside the house, where a grandfather clock chimed every hour, Granny Betty implemented her many rules on how we were to behave with the help of little homilies, and our parents became tense. There was a great deal of dark oak ceiling timbers, creaking floorboards and chunky antique furniture topped with shiny silver heirlooms, and that specific smell of much polished aged wood. Grandad and Granny Betty had lived in East Africa for many years and the house was filled with evidence of big game and souvenir hunting; animal skin rugs, an umbrella stand made from an elephant foot, fly swishes made from the tails of zebra and Masai weapons hanging on the walls. My brother and I were in turn fascinated and repelled by our grandfather's collection of 'Safari Spoils'. He had been taking part in the sport of his era, but even as a child I found it difficult to reconcile myself to the idea. I was never able to voice any disapproval or to ask too many questions however. Grandad was rather gruff and would very easily 'fly off the handle' if crossed, but I wish I'd been brave enough to do so.

Granddad had been taken prisoner of war early on in World War One, earning status amongst his fellow prisoners by escaping (and getting recaptured) several times. After repatriation, he joined the Colonial Office, married the genteel daughter of a local clergyman, our grandmother Melessina, then sailed out to Tanganyika in East Africa where they remained posted until the beginning of World War Two. Like us, they would sail back to the UK on leave every two or three years, returning to East Africa after each visit.

Our father was born on one such visit, in the home of his grandparents in Norfolk, and two years later, his sister, Joan. Returning to East Africa each time, the two children lived an entitled existence for eight years, being cared for by African Ayahs (Nannies) and occasionally travelling and moving around the Tanganyika Territories with their parents.

But when Father and his sister were eight and six respectively, the family sailed once more to England where both children were then left to be educated at boarding schools. Neither of them ever lived with their parents again. Instead, our father spent school holidays with his father's sister, his Aunt Wanda, who lived in Cornwall with her husband and three daughters. She became his surrogate mother and his times spent there constituted the happiest of his childhood. His sister, meanwhile, didn't fare so well, instead spending her school holidays with a variety of unrelated host families.

Our paternal grandparents went on to have a further daughter, Jill, but after returning to the UK at the outbreak of war, they effectively separated. Grandad worked in Intelligence during the war, based in Cairo and travelling around the Middle East and, like our maternal grandfather, much of what he did remains a mystery.

Our grandmother Melessina meanwhile, took on the job as a housemistress in a boarding school where Jill was able to live with her. She'd had an easy life until then, and no doubt the next few years of financial and physical hardship, combined with a congenital heart problem, contributed to her early death. I never knew her. After her death, our grandfather married Betty, who had been Melesina's best friend in Tanganyika and with whom he had been having a relationship for many years.

I have always valued family stories, the handing down of what we know about our ancestors from one generation to the next. That the stories will only tell us a fraction about who our ancestors really were as people, and that they will be coloured and flawed by each retelling, is sadly inevitable, but that they will be kept alive is something I consider of more importance. I am lucky enough to come from a family who has preserved a good deal of knowledge about its forebears, much of it in diaries as well as photographs. Perhaps, as in ancient times, it's the role of the mother to keep them alive for every subsequent generation, and perhaps that's what I'm doing by writing this account of my childhood. Certainly my own mother was always a great teller of stories, imaginary and factual. She could weave tales of ghostly ships or strange happenings that kept my brother and me and often many of our childhood friends entertained and clutching onto each other in the dark. And she could just as easily hold us spellbound with the highly descriptive telling of stories about her own childhood and the lives of her parents and grandparents. I was brought up with these stories and for this reason, the few facts of my grandparent's past that I include here are, for me, just part of who we all are.

Us with Grandad at Pond Cottage, Henley

Mark

I don't think that I've met a fellow human who doesn't harbour some regrets trawled from their childhood. One of mine is not getting to know our paternal grandfather better. He was a scary old man with a fascinating past. Participated in both World Wars, taken prisoner at the Somme and escaping several times before finally managing to reach freedom days before the Armistice, which I take to be extremely prescient.

We were posted to Lebanon after Hong Kong and as I am still drifting through memorial fog at this stage, I won't attempt detail!

Lebanon (1957 & 1958)

Our house in Shemlan

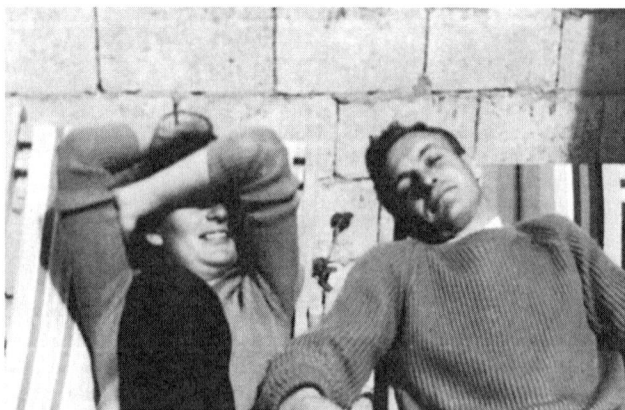

Mother and Father

Philippa

The house provided for us was a typical Lebanese village home. It was built into the hillside and backed by a steep rock face. Stone steps led up the side of the house to the flat roof, the only access to an attic room. On the ground floor, a deep covered terrace kept the house cool in summer. In the garden, tall trees added dappled shade, and a swing hung from the branches of a walnut tree. Sitting on the swing, I could watch columns of tiger ants marching up the trunk. If I wiped my finger across their path, they would stop and congregate at the point at which I'd broken their route, taking their time to negotiate the invisible blockade.

A gate beside the walnut tree opened onto a narrow track. If we went up the hill, we came to the village road, along which Mr Hitti sold provisions from an old garage. Down the hill, it led to a lesser road that wound dustily through the tiny houses below us, where village children played and dogs and chickens roamed. From time to time, Arab hunters passed along the track. They carried their guns with considerable bravado, and the more songbirds that dangled bloodily from their belts, the greater their pride.

With only unleavened bread available from the village, Mother made all our bread. She would stand at a table set up on the terrace to knead the dough, her movements rhythmic and hypnotic to watch, her young arms smooth, strong and brown. She also perfected the art of making croissants. Mother had been born and brought up in Hungary and favoured meals that were far removed from the usual English diet of the day. Always keen to experiment, she was taught to cook Lebanese food by a young woman from the village called Jacqueline who helped her in the house, long before mediocre versions of such foods became known in the UK,

Jacqueline introduced Mother and us to Lebanese dishes such as Tabbouleh, made from moistened bulgar wheat laden with copious amounts of onion, parsley and mint and rich in the flavours of lemon juice and olive oil; Hummus, made by mashing chick peas and sesame paste together to make a thick and creamy dip well laced with garlic, olive oil and lemon juice; and Stuffed Vine Leaves, using leaves from the grape vines in our garden rolled tightly around a rice based mixture and steamed until soft. Many of the Lebanese dishes Mother learnt to cook at that time became permanent family favourites and I still use the recipes she carefully wrote down to this day.

In the absence of an English speaking school nearby, Mother joined the PNEU (Parents National Education Union) and embraced home education. Mark, being two and a half years younger than me and only four, attended 'nursery school' at the home of the MECAS director's wife who minded the younger children, whilst Mother taught me and a few of the other older children of Father's fellow students. We sat under the walnut tree and applied ourselves diligently to the lessons shipped out from the UK; arithmetic, spelling, nature study and physical education. The latter required us to play 'catch' with beanbags, which Mother made from scraps of material stuffed with dried chickpeas.

Whilst moving home and country every two or three years wasn't conducive to responsible pet ownership, our mother nevertheless attracted them and we seemed to end up with a variety of rescued animal companions in most of the countries we lived in. Having to leave them behind caused considerable heartache, and it would no doubt have been wiser never to take them on. But for Mother, much as for me, a life without animals was never on the cards.

When we first arrived in Shemlan one of the wives of an outgoing 'student' at the language school pleaded with Mother to take her cat, another victim of the vagaries of army life. Mother had been looking forward to a day's shopping in Beirut and had booked herself a seat on the Landrover that went down to the city once a week. Feeling reluctant to cancel the trip, she suggested putting the cat on the roof of our house until she came home, where it could find shelter from the sun in the attic. She wondered whether it would take itself into the hills whilst she was away, but when she returned home she found it was still there, waiting patiently and calmly for its new owner. Mother named him Pushkin.

Then Little Stick arrived. Our parents couldn't afford, or didn't think they needed, a car and when one of the Arab Porters from the language school told Mother about a donkey he knew of called Little Stick who needed a home, she didn't hesitate in offering him one. Little Stick had recently completed a journey around the Middle East with an English journalist, the porter told us. We were never able to verify this story, but it is a good one, and provides an evocative picture of his previous life. Man and donkey trudging together through the ancient landscape. Mother paid £12 for Little Stick and brought him home, where he became a willing and much loved mode of transport for our family. But not without a few initial teething problems! Little Stick was a very large, very strong Jack donkey, and our mother was very slight.

Cut into the hillside on a lower level, and accessible from our garden down some steep steps, was an old store shed. This was Little Stick's winter stable. In the summer, and during the day, he was tethered to graze in the garden when he wasn't in use. But the struggle that took place every morning as Mother attempted to put on his headcollar and bring him up into the garden became increasingly desperate, neither party prepared to surrender to the other. The problem proved to be oats!

With no previous experience of keeping equines, Mother had dutifully bought a large sack of energy giving oats, a serving of which she gave to Little Stick every morning. But after seeking the advice of a friend who had kept horses, Mother subsequently discovered that Little Stick was much better behaved without oats. He had no doubt needed them to give him energy on his epic journey, but for his more sedentary lifestyle as our taxi, they provided him with more energy than he needed. From then on, he fed on grass and hay and became much easier to handle.

The sack of oats meanwhile remained in a corner of the shed where, as the weeks went by, Mother noticed it getting emptier by the day. On closer inspection she found a long and energetic column of tiger ants leading to and from the sack. The column forged under the door from the store shed, up the stone steps and through the garden in the direction of the walnut tree, each departing ant weighed down by a single oat.

Wash down for Little Stick

Walking in the hills

*Mother cuts a hole in the top of an orange and pushes a
sugar lump firmly down through the flesh. She gives one each
to Mark and me and we suck the juice out through the sugar.
It's a messy business and we have to be outside for this treat.
We offer sugar lumps to Little Stick, but he pushes our hands
away with his nose. He wants the orange. So Mother cuts an
orange into wedges for us to feed to him, one at a time. He
squelches noisily with his eyes half closed, the juices flowing
freely out of his mouth and the citrus smell strong in the warm
air. He is keen for more. We forget to straighten our hands as
we feed him and he nips our wrinkled palms in his enthusiasm.*

I believe the posting in Shemlan was one of the happiest
for our parents. They were young and beautiful and whatever
life threw at them was an adventure. They made new friends
in the small expat community and gave parties in the large
stone floored living room, cigarette smoke and music drifting
out into the night air. There were sunny, sweet smelling walks
up rough mountain tracks, and picnics beside clear running
streams, often accompanied by other families. Little Stick was
always with us, more fun than any car, and we took turns to
ride on his bony back. We walked around the ancient Roman
columns at Baalbek, and through the great Cedar forests high
up in the hills. Our birthday parties came and went and Father
earned cult status with all the children by doing magic tricks
involving matchboxes and eggs in glasses of water.

For my seventh birthday, Mother sewed matching party
dresses for my favourite doll and me in pale blue taffeta. She
made all our clothes, and on this occasion we went down to
Beiruit to buy me matching shoes. My birthday is just before

58

Christmas and it grew increasingly cold as we wound our way back up the steep winding road to Shemlan. It would snow the next day. But on that evening the sky was clear, and through the back window of the car the receding lights of the city below us quickly gave way to the more insistent intensity of stars.

Jacqueline told Mother about a litter of puppies in a neighbouring village that were being persecuted by local children. This would not have been an unusual occurrence. There were dozens of stray 'pie-dogs' in every village and countless acts of cruelty directed towards animals every day. But something made this occasion one time too many. Mother saddled up Little Stick and rode off down the rough road.

She found the puppies quite easily. A group of children were playing football with one of them. She shouted at the children and they ran away. As they did so, the mother dog dashed out of hiding and grabbed one of the puppies. She ran with it in her mouth and disappeared up the hillside. Mother didn't see it again. But she picked up the remaining two puppies and took them home. Another English family from MECAS adopted one, and we kept the other. We called her Pie Dog. It seemed fitting. She was tiny and frightened, but with love, good food and gentle handling, she was on her way to becoming quite a large and well adjusted dog by the time we were forced to evacuate from Shemlan in June 1958.

By this time conflict had escalated between Lebanese Muslims who wanted Lebanon to join the newly formed United Arab Republic with Egypt and Syria, and the Maronite Christians who wanted to maintain an alliance with Western powers. The UK was neutral in this crisis and we were not seen as enemies. But then, for several nights running, gunfire had echoed around the surrounding hills. And as Shemlan became a battleground for Syrian backed rebels fighting governmental troops, Syrian troops began to use the roof of our house as a command post.

"You are safe with us here. We will protect you," they told us. Father had translated the Arabic for us, proud of his newfound command of the language.

But that night, a new guard is posted on the roof. He hears a rustling noise in the garden and shouts out a question. There is no answer but the rustling continues. He lifts his gun to take aim and stares into the darkness, all senses focused on the source. Eventually, his eyes find the white tips of two long ears and he fires.

Little Stick is shaken by last night's barrage of bullets that holed his metal water bucket, but is otherwise unscathed. Mother is grooming him. He likes it and begins to relax.

"He's made of tough stuff," my father remarks the next morning, having sorted things out with the Syrian guards. He sounds proud.

A soldier gazes down at us impassively from the roof. He is clutching a Bazooka and smoking a cigarette. Then the director of MECAS arrives. He tells us that the Foreign Office is closing MECAS.

"The Syrians have taken Shemlan," he says, "and all British Nationals are being instructed to leave. We are giving everyone twenty-four hours to evacuate, during which time you will be provided with a guard." He nods his head towards the roof of our house. "Then you'll be taken down to Beirut.

You'll be safer there and we can get you out easily. Probably to Cyprus."

Mother is listening and sets her mouth stubbornly. We know that look.

"I have animals to consider," she says. "I won't leave them."

Father looks embarrassed. But in the end, it is arranged that we will travel north instead, away from the fighting, to Farayah. The director knows the proprietor of a small hotel there.

"Selim Debs is a good man and you'll be safe there for a while with your animals, until we know what to do with you."

The MECAS porter who sold Mother Little Stick has agreed to re-home him for her and has sent instruction to my mother to go to the next village of Souk-El-Gharb, where his brother will meet her and take the donkey. Father is being de-briefed at MECAS so we stay with a tearful Jacqueline whilst Mother prepares to take Little Stick to safety.

She ties a piece of white cloth to a stick and, knowing Syrian forces are holed up in the hills all around, she holds this high above her head as she and Little Stick take their last walk together. In Souk-al-Garb, she hands him over to the porter's brother who takes off the beaded rope headcollar with hanging tassels that he always wore, and replaces it with something more basic with a metal nose-band.

He hands the rope headcollar to Mother who holds little Little Stick's huge head for a few moments, then turns and walks back to Shemlan on her own. She never finds out what happens to him after that, but for over half a century, she keeps his head collar hanging on the wall of her home in Hampshire where it still evokes powerful memories.

We travel in a black car flying two flags from its bonnet. One is the Union Jack and the other is white.

"I need to wee-wee," Mark announces.

We stop and climb the rocky scrubland beside the road for a few yards where we all take the opportunity to relieve ourselves. Suddenly, Father shouts out.

"What the blazers do you think you are doing, Mark?"

We all look at Mark, then follow Father's gaze to the car below us. On the back window ledge, his popgun lies in full view. Father leaps down the slope and pulls the gun from sight.

"We could have all been killed," he says.

As the fighting in the Lebanon continued and MECAS remained closed, we lived a curiously charmed life in Farayah whilst the powers that be decided what to do with us. Eventually, we were ordered down to Beirut to await transport to Cyprus. Selim Debs had fallen in love with Pie Dog and was very willing to give her a home. Our mother only agreed if he took Pushkin as well and I remember her visible distress as we left for Beirut.

We looked out of the back window of the car and saw the landlord watching us go, with Pie Dog standing at his side. Mother cried silently, her hands over her mouth and her eyes spilling over. Sometime later, she heard that Pushkin had been run over shortly after our departure, but that Pie Dog was leading a happy life in the mountains.

After a military coup in Iraq toppled the pro west government in July of that same year, the Lebanese President requested urgent American military assistance against possible threats from Syria and Egypt as well as from the internal opposition. America sent a large naval fleet and over twenty thousand troops to Beirut, but managed to instigate a diplomatic end to the conflict and withdrew in October of the same year. MECAS opened its doors once again, but by then, we had moved on.

Saying Goodbye to 'Pie Dog' and 'Pushkin' in Faraya

Cyprus (1958)

Me and Father before he left for Jordan

On arriving in Cyprus, we were billeted in the half deserted Dome Hotel in Kyrenia, once a popular holiday destination in the north of the island. Father had been given leave and our parents were looking forward to us all being able to explore as much of that beautiful island as possible during our short time there. And this we did. There are photos of us all visiting Hilarion Castle near Kyrenia, the village of Bellapain and eventually Nicosia, but it can't have been very easy.

Cyprus at that time, much like the rest of the Middle East that year, was in a state of emergency. There were curfews in many of the towns to protect the public, and British families around the island had been placed under the protection of the army. Kyrenia was historically a Turkish town, but the majority of the population at that time was Greek and the increasing danger to British families and personnel was that of being attacked by Greek extremists who sought independence from Britain. Once again, I turn to the history books for further enlightenment. The disturbances in Cyprus seem to have been ongoing throughout my life and I want to remind myself of their roots

Originally occupied by Greeks, Cyprus was invaded and fought over from ancient times to the middle ages. The Ottoman Empire finally gained control over the island in 1570 and the Turkish population on the island grew, as did disturbances and aggression between the Christian Greek population and the Muslim Turks.

In 1878, the Ottoman Empire leased Cyprus to the British on the understanding that Britain would offer assistance against any attack from Russia. The British established a naval and military base in Cyprus, and at the outbreak of World War One, when Turkey chose to fight on the side of Germany and Greece chose to remain neutral, Cyprus was formerly annexed by Britain as a Crown Colony and the country became an important strategic British Military Base during both world wars.

Following World War Two, Britain rejected demands from both Turkey and Greece for the island to be given to them and continued to govern a relatively peaceful mixed population of Greek and Turkish Cypriots. By 1955 however, a Greek nationalistic organisation called EOKA began to make demands for the withdrawal of the British and a hand over of the island to Greece.

After a series of terrorist attacks on the British by EOKA, the British Government initially reacted by deporting the leaders of the movement. But by 1958, EOKA had regrouped and was intensifying a campaign of guerilla warfare against the British, as well as brutal intimidation of the Greek population to ensure their support. When rumours of attacks on Turks by EOKA began to spread, the Turkish population retaliated with a series of violent reprisals against the Greeks. They demanded that the country be partitioned into separate Turkish and Greek zones, and to this end Greek properties were looted and burned and businesses destroyed, fuelling a growing hatred between the two communities who had previously been friends and neighbours. In the ensuing battles, there were countless murders and atrocities committed on all sides, and hundreds of British soldiers were ambushed and killed over the period, the vast majority of whom had only been conscripted to Cyprus for the duration of their national service.

We are on the beach in Kyrenia overlooking the harbour, Mother, Father, Mark and I. We have a rubber bucket with swirly colours and a matching spade that bends, but with which we hope to make sandcastles. The sea is flat and iridescent in the bright sunlight. Alongside us is a pontoon that reaches out from the shore towards a collection of small brightly coloured fishing boats floating motionless in the water. Father is holding a snorkeling mask and wants to show me how to use it. We walk together into the water until it reaches my waist. Then he helps me stretch the mask over my head. The rubber on the strap catches my hair and it hurts.

I'm not feeling very enthusiastic, but my father is a determined man.

"Now take a deep breath and put your face into the water," he says.

This proves a difficult combination and at first I can only stare into the water for a few seconds at a time. I see nothing as the mask keeps filling with water and I panic. Eventually, however, Father's perseverance is rewarded. I master the technique of pressing the mask onto my face to squeeze out all the air to seal the edges, and I see the kaleidoscopic underwater world around my feet for the first time. The fish, that look like briefly glimpsed blurred paint splats from the surface, become crystal clear and there are myriads of them, in all colours, some nibbling at my toes. I am entranced and my father and I grin at each other in delight each time I come up for air.

Father eventually received his orders, which were to go to Jordan, unaccompanied. A military coup in Iraq had destroyed the newly formed Arab Union between Jordan and Iraq and Jordan had found itself isolated. Fearing internal discontent, as well as possible threat from Egypt, King Hussein of Jordan had accepted British and American presence to lend strength and stability to the government. Father was to be a part of that presence and presumably of greater value on account of his being able to speak Arabic. Mother, Mark and I, on the other hand, were to be flown home and we were all in a sombre mood as we were driven to a hotel in Nicosia to await the next flights out.

The low sun is in our faces as we sit chatting quietly on the balcony of our hotel in Nicosia. We are all smiling and Mother takes some photographs. But nothing feels quite right. Father is in uniform. He is due to leave shortly to get on a plane and fly to Jordan. Mother, Mark and I are flying back to England in the morning. Suddenly the sirens wail, making us all jump, and down below us people begin to rush towards their destinations, anxious to get off the streets. This is our cue to stay inside until the sirens sound again in the morning.

We leave the balcony and move back into the room where Father becomes brisk and detached. He opens a drawer and takes out a pistol and a leather holster on a strap. He loops the holster over his shoulder to fit under his arm and buckles the straps around his middle. He wears this under his shirt. Now he checks the mechanisms of the gun and slips it into the holster, out of sight. Mark is entranced and asks all the pertinent questions about ammunition that a five year old knows to ask, before Father hugs us all and goes out.

We left Cyprus then, although six years later our family was tenuously involved in the island once again. I'm jumping ahead here. But the conflict in Cyprus remained unchanged over the interim years. The Greek Cypriots continued to demand Greek rule and eventually the Turkish Cypriots turned to Turkey for military support. The British Government then instigated urgent discussions with Greece, Turkey and the Cypriot communities in an attempt to find a solution to the escalating crisis that was threatening international security. Finally, in 1960, Cyprus was declared an independent Republic with both Greek and Turkish administrators, and with Britain continuing to control two military bases on the island.

After independence however, the allocated division of power in Cyprus was considered unjust by both Turkish and Greek Cypriots and tensions between the two communities continued to fester. In December 1963 violence erupted and resulted in horrific tales of mass murders, retaliations and misplacements of both sides by the other.

Most affected were Turkish Cypriots and, when Turkey threatened military intervention, the United Nations decided to send a peacekeeping force to Cyprus in an attempt to quell the situation. They would go on to create a buffer zone that effectively divided the country in half, with the Turks in the north and the Greeks in the south, but first they needed manpower to swell the ranks of the multinational force. And in 1964 our father was given immediate orders to don the iconic United Nations blue beret and go to Cyprus to join them.

We were living in Malta at the time, where Father had a public relations post, and we were to remain there to await his return.

It is a Sunday morning in Malta, not long after Father left for Cyprus, and the iconic sound of the bells of Mosta Dome ring out monotonously as Mother and I walk down the dusty street from our house to the local village store. I am now thirteen and Mother is thirty-seven. The door of the store is open as usual and piles of newspapers and magazines tied up with string spill over the floor and out onto the street. There really is nowhere else to stack them as the store is packed from floor to ceiling with products! You can buy anything from pencils to washing powder here. We pick our way carefully to the counter.

"Good morning, Mr Gatt," my mother says in greeting.

"Good morning, Mrs Hilpern," comes the greeting back, but Mr Gatt is frowning. He nervously indicates the front page of the Sunday Express.

"But you have not seen the paper this morning, Mrs Hilpern," he says.

We look down in horror. Father's face is taking up the first half of the front page. And the story headline was printed in bold;

'THEN YOU'D BETTER SHOOT, SAYS THE MAJOR"

It appeared that Father's convoy had been stopped at a roadblock manned by a group of Greek insurgents and that they had threatened him with shooting if he continued on his way. According to the Sunday Express,

The Major took his pipe out of his mouth and said, "Then you'd better shoot!"

It was exactly the sort of challenging comment Father would have made and we had no doubt that he would have had every intention of calling their bluff. However, he and his convoy were prevented from doing so and were held captive under a makeshift awning by the roadside.

Back in England, where my brother was by then at boarding school, the headmaster called him into his study to inform him that his father had been taken prisoner and to prepare himself for the worst! I don't know how long it took for the information to filter back to England, but luckily, the drama was comparatively short-lived. Father and his convoy were released after a few hours of negotiations and, as he said he would do, he was allowed to continue on his way!

Benenden Uk (1958-1959)

Father in Jordan

With Billie in Benenden

After we left Cyprus in 1958, Mother, Mark and I lived for the next ten months in the heart of the Kent countryside near Benenden, where Mother had rented in a tiny thatched cottage.

I don't really know what actual role our father played in Jordan, but it would seem that he covered great distances. There are photographs of him with the Bedouin in the desert around Kerak near the Dead Sea, in which he appears very much at ease. He grew to have a great deal of respect for these nomadic people of the desert. Other photographs show him and fellow officers with the Jordanian Police and their camels many miles further north at the fortress in Azraq, a remote and ancient settlement built around the only oasis within twelve thousand miles of desert. And I can imagine he was thrilled to be there. It was Azraq where T. E. Lawrence had made his headquarters during the Arab Revolt of 1916 and my father was a great admirer of the man and his book. *The Seven Pillars of Wisdom* was a tome that travelled around the world with us. I doubt Father was merely retracing the historic footsteps of his idol however. With his newly gained knowledge of Arab culture and language, I imagine he was a useful ear to the ground in whatever role he played. But his photographs do give a hint of what it meant to him to be there. He wears the Arab headdress in many of them and full Arab dress when with the Jordanian Police. I can only speculate as to why. But I do believe he would have been drinking in his first experience of the people, their customs and the extraordinary landscape of the desert, as well as doing the job he was sent to do. For the rest of his life, his passion for the desert and the old ways of the Arab world was the mainstay of his career.

That winter in England was cold with lots of snow. Mother continued to teach us through the PNEU, and she had her army housekeeping allowance with which she was just about able to make ends meet. I remember hot pots and stews, things on toast and hearty puddings – English food to keep us warm. Early on, she went to the local garage to buy a car, negotiating a deal to pay for it in monthly instalments. I think the car was an old Austin, dark green with leather seats. We christened it 'Juggins' and the car became our ticket to freedom.

Juggins had no heating so Mother would provide hot water bottles and a blanket for longer journeys. But first, she had to start the engine, easing out the choke and swearing under her breath when the engine failed to turn over. More often than not she had to get out and crank start the engine, inserting the bent metal handle into a mysterious cavity in the front of the car and exerting a huge amount of physical effort to turn the engine over, her breath rising up in steamy clouds from the front of the car.

The bell above the door of the village store in Benenden clangs as we walk in. There are a few other people in a queue and everyone turns around as we go in. The smell of polished wood mixes with that of the myriad of fresh foods on display. Mother nods in greeting as we wait. The shop has shelves from floor to ceiling and stocks everything a household needs.

Mark and I poke at each other behind our mother's back. Then it's our turn and Mother greets the grocer who is standing behind the high wooden counter. We hoist ourselves up onto the stools in front of the counter and swing our legs. Mother starts to read out her list, one item at a time, and the grocer fetches each thing she asks for and places it on the counter. Sometimes he has to use his stepladder to reach. Mother's list comes to an end and the grocer adds up the total cost. We have pins and needles in our legs by now and need to jump down. But we know we must wait.

"Please put it on my account," says Mother, as she loads all the items into her basket. Now we can get down.

"Good-day!" we all say.

We go out, our feet prickly and numb and the bell clangs again. Juggins is parked outside and we all pile in.

The main charm of the cottage for Mark and me was the steeply sloping floor of our bedroom. Covered with lino it made a wonderful slippery slide to race down on our bottoms. We slept in two single beds placed end to end and were always allowed a 'five minute talk' in the dark before we went to sleep. We began to create an imaginary world for ourselves, inventing a variety of events and people with which we had fun for much of our childhood.

We also developed the habit of rocking ourselves to sleep, a very hypnotic and comforting process but one that no doubt caused our mother some concern, not least because of the tangles in our hair the next morning! And Mark began to suffer with night terrors, during which he would wake up screaming and inconsolable. These went on for a few years and our mother, and father when he was around, would try to wake him up and comfort him but it always took a long time.

I, meanwhile, would wake in the middle of the night to the sensation of someone tickling me and calling my name. Mother assumed we were in need of a tonic and gave us Bemax and Virol and cod liver oil every morning! Mark's night terrors continued for some years, but my nighttime experiences only happened in that cottage. I often wonder if the house was haunted by a restless being which attached itself onto the two children who slept in its room! Or maybe I had just listened to too many of my mother's stories.

Our neighbour was a Mrs Ayla Hannay who was also an expat from the Middle East. She had arrived soon after we had, moving into the other half of our cottage with her mother and two huge white shaggy dogs, one of which had only three legs. Mark and I were a little in awe of them. We were regularly invited for tea on Sundays and allowed to watch Mrs Hannay's television, something we had never seen before.

The Lone Ranger became our favourite, and other 'Westerns', one of whose accompanying music was Dvorjaks New World Symphony which, when I hear it today, still transports me to the world of 'Cowboys and Indians' and Mrs Hannay's warm sitting room.

We drive to Tenterden in Juggins to do some Christmas shopping. Mother helps Mark and me buy each other's Christmas present in the toyshop and we are bursting with excitement when we go to bed that night.

"I bet you can't guess what I've bought you for Christmas?" Mark challenges me in loud whisper.

76

More than anything I want another hand puppet to boost my growing collection, so I say the first thing that comes into my head.

"A puppet?"

Mark bursts into noisy tears and Mother comes in to see what is the matter. She's angry with us for playing the guessing game and for guessing and spoiling the surprise. The next day we go back to Tenterden and Mark is made to take the puppet back and swap it for something else instead. I don't remember what it was.

I remember Father being with us briefly in Benenden, maybe for Christmas? The photos show that it was cold. On returning from Jordan I assume he must have had leave. But then he, being a gunner, had been required to go to Infantry Training School in Warminster before taking up his next post, which was to command an infantry battalion in Aden.

In the meantime, Billie came to stay with increasing regularity. Irreparable cracks were appearing in her marriage, which meant she needed to get away. And although she and Mother had long and intense whispered conversations about Jack, Billie's visits also meant our mother laughed a lot and we always loved her coming.

Another visitor to our cottage one day was a fellow army officer who had been on board the Asturius. I learnt in later years that he and Mother had become close at the time. But I remember how his visit caused Mother and Billie much embarrassed hilarity after he'd left. We discarded the incident at the time, but much later, well after we had grown up, the lifelong infatuation this man had for my mother, and the tenacity of his pursuit at a time she was most vulnerable, played a vital role in the breakup of our parent's marriage. But that story is for later.

As the winter gave way to spring, we explored the lanes, hedgerows and woods around us and I remember it as a very happy time. I believe the seeds were sown back then for my love of the English countryside.

Finally, with his training completed, Father was given his orders to fly out to Aden. He was to go on ahead and sort out our living accommodation, and we were to follow by sea.

We set sail on the Nevasa, a small ship displaying the iconic blue line of the British forces troopships around its hull. I was eight and a half and Mark was six.

HMT Nevasa

Aden (1959-1960)

The Arab situation in any area of the Middle East was, and still is, a complexity I have no wish to try and unravel here. Suffice it to say that Aden, a port at the base of the Arab Peninsular surrounded by a fairly small area of barren, volcanic land, had been a British Colony since 1839.

A geographically vital stop off point for trade between Britain and the Far East, it became a port of huge importance to the British, especially after the opening of the Suez Canal in 1869 and, by the middle of the 20th century, Aden's oil refinery constituted all British oil interests in the area as well as providing virtually the sole support system to the local economy.

The lands around Aden consisted of traditional tribal areas ruled by Sheiks, a great many of whom, over the years, entered into loyalty treaties with the British Government. In return for British Protection, the Sheikdoms involved were allowed to retain their sovereignty and individual governmental bodies whilst agreeing to acknowledge and recognise the Colony of Aden and its harbour as part of the British Empire. This protected area became known as the Aden Protectorate and eventually extended east of Aden to the coast of the Red Sea and west to the Hadramaut.

There were other nationalistic tribes however, some from the mountainous regions beyond the Protectorate and others from the Yemen, who remained resentful of British presence in the area and regularly caused disturbances. So in order to defend the area and ensure the protection of the British forces in Aden, the Aden Protectorate Levvies (APL) had been formed in 1928, a military force made up entirely of Arab Soldiers, recruited from all over the Protectorate, under the command of Arab speaking British Officers.

By the early 1960's however, the British forces in Aden increasingly found themselves victim of deadly guerilla attacks by nationalistic liberation groups gaining support from Egypt. A state of emergency was finally declared in 1963, with British forces eventually conceding defeat and leaving Aden in 1967 when the National Liberation Front took over. But this was well after we had left.

Father arrived in Aden in the spring of 1959 to take command of his APL battalion, and to wear on his beret the APL badge of the crossed daggers of Lahej, the traditional emblem of one of the Sheikhdoms under the Aden Protectorate. Mother, Mark and I arrived in June.

We are sent to live in Sheikh Othman, a small camel station and market town on the very outskirts of the Aden Protectorate on the edge of the desert. An 'outpost' my mother calls it, where camel trains come in from the desert to unload and rest before being loaded up again and made ready to head back.

These 'ships of the desert', heavily laden and attached to each other in long lines, with their handlers riding on top or walking alongside, walk majestically and silently across the sands for days on end, heading north through the Yemen or east across the Hadramaut to trade. When a sandstorm blows in, the Arabs cover the lower half of their faces with their headdresses and the camels seal up their noses.

Father's soldiers have their own camel troop and sometimes he arranges for he and my mother to ride out on camels before the dawn when it's still cool. We are too young to go with them, but when the camels arrive at our gates, and before our parents set off, the handlers let us children have a ride.

The camels are huge and seem perpetually bad tempered, responding to whatever they are directed to do with disapproval, gargling loudly and producing a great deal of phlegm that flies out from between their teeth in spumes of froth. And when eventually they can be coerced into bending their legs to lie down or straightening them to rise to a stand, their actions are jerky and cumbersome. To be on the back of a camel when it gets up is quite a challenging experience but when we achieve it, we grin for the whole of the subsequent rolling walk around the compound.

We live in a block of four flats set within a large gated compound with a good tree to climb. The sand blows in from the desert and banks up all around. Later, Mother and Father take up archery and our compound becomes a hub of competing adults, whisky and soda in hand, whilst we children watch from the tree.

From the flat roof of our building, we can see over into the servant's quarters behind, a crowded collection of single story shacks. But we aren't allowed to look at them. Beyond them is the small dusty town, and after that the desert. We hang the washing on the roof but we can't stay up there for long. The heat is unbearable. There's a pigeon with a crooked beak up there and we feed it and give it water when we remember. We call it 'Beaky'. Sometimes Beaky comes out of the glare and down the stone stairs to the first landing to wait for us. It's cooler there.

We have a cook and a bearer who work in the kitchen. They dress in white and use the rickerty outside iron staircase that leads from the kitchen down to the servant's quarters behind the house. We are not allowed to use the stairs but if we stand at the mosquito-netting door at the top, we can watch the yellow Weaverbirds noisily building their intricate hanging nests in a dusty tree that grows beside the house.

The kitchen staff become a source of some stress to Mother, who spends a great deal of time checking up on them and often gets angry. She has to make sure that all the vegetables have been washed in Potassium Permanganate crystals to kill any bacteria or pesticides; and that the tap water has been boiled before being stored in the glass 'Gordens Dry Gin' bottles which fit flatly in rows in the door of the fridge, condensation running down over their labels every time the door is opened.

Our first cook, Ali, has a scarred face under his white turban. He seems very charming and smart and is with us for quite some time. But one day, Mother says he has stolen some teaspoons from the house so we have to get a new cook. I don't remember his name.

From the Naafi, we buy cans of condensed milk which we dilute with water to drink as there is no fresh milk available. And large gold tins of Jungle Juice, an orange powder, teaspoons of which we stir into water to make orange juice. It tastes delicious except that we have to dissolve salt tablets in it every morning to replace the salts we lose in the heat. We also have to take malaria tablets.

There are three other families living in the block. Hilary and Jane Hook live across the landing and they have a son called Simon of around our age with very blond hair. Jane is very elegant and 'does' Beauty Counselling, a type of Party Plan venture, selling make up and beauty products to other Army wives. She encourages Mother into the business and provides her with a rather smart pink beauty box filled with pink packaged products that are something quite beautiful to me. I'm not sure how committed Mother is to selling the products but she and I enjoy playing with them.

Downstairs, on one side, live Dora and Tom Todd, larger than life characters who give many loud parties attended by our parents and who feature quite regularly in the family photo albums. And downstairs on the other side are the Mattesons. I don't remember them except that they have our ginger cat when we leave Aden eighteen months later and we stay half the night with them before our night flight back to England.

Our cat is called Sissly Wissly, named after a silly Burl Ives song my parents sing together, but we call him (the cat) Gutsy for short. He had belonged to another army family before us.

Our flat in Sheikh
Othman

Mark and friend on a
camel

We visit the Souks in Crater, the main town in Aden. To reach it we have to drive along the causeway, a road built across the water connecting the northern areas of Aden, where Sheik Othman is, to the south where Crater is. The causeway is long and straight with the sea on one side and salt flats on the other where hundreds of Flamingos wade, their orange legs reflected in a mirage of salty water.

We get into the habit of stopping there to scramble on the boulders that tumble down to the sea on either side of the road. Mark and Father try to catch fish and Mother and I watch the Flamingos. We take books to read as well. I am rarely without a book on the go.

In Crater the Souks are very crowded, noisy and smelly. Mother carries a basket over her arm and moves quickly and decisively among the stalls that spill their produce and goods onto the streets. Suddenly, she sees Ali. She shouts at him and we feel very embarrassed. Ali starts to run away, but then changes his mind and stops, and Mother tells him she wants her spoons back. Ali brings them back the next day but he still gets the sack.

Us at Crater, Aden

I look at the photograph albums of our time there now and see how much we crammed into our eighteen months in Aden. By now, aged eight, I have my own camera and photo album and my childish take on things adds a new and more personal dimension to my memory bank. There are photos of camel races, tribal dances, picnic trips in dhows at sea, and endless army parades with military bands and troops of camels marching in line.

We sit under awnings at the edge of the parade ground for these latter events, and Mark and I make bets as to which soldier standing to attention is going to faint next in the heat. Parades and fainting soldiers are a regular event. Father tells us there are ways to make sure you don't faint when on parade, but the soldiers in question don't seem to know of any such technique and they are regularly carried off the parade ground with minimum interruption to the proceedings.

Some of the photos in the Aden Album taken by Father are of military trips up country into the protected areas with fellow officers. Landrovers are pictured in Lodar, parked beside groups of tribesmen in front of castellated buildings perched amongst the rocks. I've no idea what they were all doing but I imagine reconnaissance work, making sure insurgents weren't operating in the area! Without my father around to talk me through what was happening, there is a stage set quality to these pictures.

Father and Tom Todd also visited the Hadramaut at this time, establishing for Father what became a lifelong fascination with this ancient area in Southern Arabia. He visited Shabam, a town surrounded by mountains that appears to rise up from the middle of the desert, with tall narrow sandstone houses standing close together hiding dark alleyways and secret entrances through which Father took some wonderful photographs. He went back to the Hadramaut much later in his life, in another job, and spent a longer time there, working with and getting to know the people. It was a place that meant a lot to him.

In Sheikh Othman it is incredibly hot and feels threatening but I don't know why. It's probably because we are doing something out of the ordinary. Mother holds our hands very tightly as we head to the edge of the town. A roadside store spills out clay cooking pots and woven rugs and we step into the street to avoid them. A two-wheeled camel cart rattles towards the souk, and Mother pushes us back to allow it to pass. The sweet camel dung smell is momentarily overpowering. The camel has long eyelashes, crooked teeth, a peg through his nose and froth flying from his mouth. He gargles to himself and sounds angry. His wide feet, followed by the wheels of the cart, make marks in the thin layer of sand covering the street, sand that blows in from the desert at the edge of the town and gets everywhere, even through the tiniest cracks under the doors and around the windows of our flat, so that we have piles of sand in the corners of every room after a sand storm. It gets into the record player and scratches our parent's records. It gets into our hair, our ears and between our teeth. Even the water from the taps is yellow and filled with sand. And we learn to squint our eyes not just from the sun but also against the sting of flying sand that blows sharp against our bare legs and arms.

The driver sits casually on the front of the cart with his legs dangling. He looks at us briefly. He's chewing Khat and shoots out a jet of green spittle to land in the dust. Other men along the street squat in doorways or stand around in groups, seemingly with nothing to do and it's hard not to believe that they too are staring at us, the only Europeans around. They wear Foutah's, cotton fabric wound around their middle and rolled at the top to secure into a short skirt, and shirts, with turbans wound around their heads. There are women here too, shrouded in black purdah, moving down the street in groups like flocks of black crows, their faceless voices pitched high and shrill. Somewhere behind us a dog barks and others join in. There are packs of wild dogs in the town and we have been told to keep away from them. We hear *them outside our gates at night, their howls mingling with the yelps of the hyenas further out in the desert. Father has a curious dislike of hyenas and swears when he hears them. I don't know why. We reach our destination, a door in the street much like any other. Mother checks the address and knocks.*

Female voices ululate in greeting as we climb narrow stairs to sit around the edges of a dimly lit room. The arab wives of the APL soldiers have removed their purdah and are dressed in rich colours with armfuls of jangling bangles. The smell of coffee combines with their hauntingly sweet perfume. From a table in the middle of the room, the coffee is poured from a height into tiny cups and offered around with bowls of Halva, my first experience of both.

We can't understand what they say but in the universal language of mime, the women laugh when I first taste the strong sweet coffee. I can't help but grimace before gratefully accepting a piece of Halva to take the taste away. The women touch my face and hair and present me with a small black lacey scarf that holds onto the memory of their scent down the years.

We had to go to school in Aden, a quadrangle of single storey classrooms built around a central playground with deep verandahs around the edges providing shade. I only remember my first day with any clarity as I was sent out of the classroom for not knowing the teacher's name and calling her 'Miss'! A harsh introduction to formal schooling!

There are vague memories of Brownies and Ballet classes after that, with photos to back them up, and a teacher I liked getting married and changing her name. But as ever, my main memories are of family events. And true to form, as a family we explored as much as we could within the confines of the Aden Protectorate, either in our family car, a yellow 'Taunus', (Isabella by model and by name – we still named our cars) or by army Landrover. Father always had a driver on hand to take us on the more rugged journeys when he was on leave.

I think much of our life in Aden must have been synonymous with trying to combat the extreme heat. Sheikh Othman boasted recreational gardens that we visited often, a small well-watered leafy sanctuary at the edge of the village with extraordinary flowers whose names I still don't know and where a little primitive farm of chickens, goats and oxen, and a cage of monkeys, flourished in the comparative cool.

School finished at lunchtime and everyone would flock to the sea to cool off. Swimming at Gold Mour, an Army Lido and Club, was a daily ritual. There was an area for 'Officers' and their families and another separate area for 'Other Ranks'. The swimming area with its diving boards was communal however. It was netted off from sharks, and holes in the netting caused by Sting Rays were a constant threat. When the tide went out, the area was reduced to a sludge that writhed with stranded mini creatures, including fat sea slugs who lay helplessly on what had been the ocean floor. I have a lasting horror of these poor things being used as water pistols by boys against us girls.

But there were many happier memories made at Gold Mour; all of us sitting on the plastic chairs that left wields on your back and legs; Mark and I learning to dive and peeling the sunburn of one another's noses; Mother and Father laughing with friends, or with each other, as they viewed their fellow sun worshippers and made the occasional acerbic comment; us drinking 7UP and eating bacon sandwiches with tomato ketchup from the café which was a great treat.

Another cool off point was the RAF beach at Khormaksar. a large expanse of sand open to the sea where you could sometimes catch a breeze. We walked along its length and drew pictures in the sand.

But our favourite place to go was Bir Fukum, an army tented retreat pitched on the beach far west of Aden along the coast and where we spent many happy weekends. The journey there was long and dusty, the road roughly cut through the mountains. We were driven in the Landrovers, often a convoy of us leaving clouds of yellow dust behind us, and to this day the smell and sound of the engines of these faithful vehicles take me back to those bumpy journeys.

I think we were very much allowed to run wild at Bir Fukum whilst our parents swam and drank and played the music of the times. The open sided 'mess tents' had generators rumbling behind and were equipped with record players as well as fridges and cookers, from where the Arab bearers prepared meals and topped up the drinks. There were always many children of our own age to play with and we had our own games to play.

The army tents in which we slept were huge, a double layer of khaki canvas (another smell memory!) held up with one or two poles in the centre. Having chosen our camp beds, we children would clamber between the two layers of the tent and attempt to climb up to the pole at the top where there was a hole through which we could see down into the tent. Then we'd slide back down the dark canvas cavity to the bottom.

This kept us busy for ages! And wo betide any adult who came into the tent! They would never know who might be spying on them from above!

But it's the night times I remember the most. As we lay in our camp beds and the noise of the adults' partying faded, the swishing sound of the tiny waves lapping onto the course sand was joined by an insistent clicking noise as millions of hermit crabs came out of the sea and clambered up and along the beach doing whatever it was they did at night.

We had good friends, the Lloyds, who lived in Lahej, in the neighbouring Sheikhdom. Lahej was about an hour's drive away from Aden in the Landrovers as I remember it. It was cooler up there and there were more trees. The Lloyds lived in an old palace that had once belonged to Sultan of Lahej. We children played amongst the Lion cages, long emptied of their sad occupants, nestled amongst the vast jungle of their garden. 'Tiny', their daughter, was my best friend, she and I having bonded over our joint collection of child sized bangles that you could buy from the souk. They were gaudy, gold painted plastic but we loved them and were determined to have them all the way up our arms.

I can't remember why, but Mark and I once stayed on our own overnight with her family and I had my first ever experience of homesickness, watching the shadows made by the trees outside the window playing on the wall through the mosquito netting over my bed, willing the morning to come and my parents to return.

Mark

Aden, and the mist is slowly lifting. Living on the edge of the desert involved sand and heat! Our ceiling fans had three speeds I remember. Those weekend trips to the beach at Beir Fukam and sleeping in Bell Tents; tipsy parents; and the long drive home in the back of the Landrover, the whine of the differential sending us into a trance, and a billboard hovering above a roadside café close to home looking like the moon with Coca Cola written on it.

In the NAAFI, where a grey metal radio was bolted to the wall continually tuned to BFBS, you could get baked beans and cornflakes and bottles of Fanta from a newfangled vending machine, the first we'd ever seen.

And across the sea from the causeway, Slave Island shimmered. Here was where they built dhows using wooden dowels with nary a steel or iron nail which meant they had a very long life.

I fell one night bouncing on my bed, nearly losing an eye on the corner of the bedside table. The MO who stitched me up was dragged out of the mess, drunk. My mother fainted as with needle in his shaking hand he approached my eye. He did a good job though.

Another time I fished off the causeway wearing wet flip-flops and sliced through my foot on a broken 7UP bottle. I had to wear my mother's leather archery arm protector strapped onto my foot for weeks.

In hindsight, I was somewhat accident-prone but have no recollection of consciously taking unnecessary risks. I think I thought that whatever went wrong, someone would be around to fix it. I actually learnt to dive before I could swim from the greatest of heights, confident that rescue would be at hand. And it always was.

My father used to appear of an evening when not on exercise, sun burned and dusty and a spring in his step, pipe in mouth. He loved soldiering, camels and Arabs more or less in that order and I'm sure his family slotted in there somewhere. Apart from a short break as a shoe salesman, he had been in the army since 1944, landed on Swordfish Beach on D Day, served in Korea, Cyprus and Oman, and other places unknown as a combat officer.

On the Causeway

There was only one occasion many many years later that he spoke to me of his experiences in what I'm sure was merely a precis format, but it took a shared bottle of whisky to eek it out of him and most of the night. I actually have Spielberg to thank for that as it was only after I dragged him to see *Saving Private Ryan* that he opened the door a chink. He told me the sound of rounds hitting the landing craft at the start of the film got to him and made him lower his guard.

Philippa

As it was in the Army, much of our parent's social life centred around private parties as well as formal regimental occasions and, as the wife of an army officer, wherever we were in the world our mother threw the requisite parties in great style. She was a wonderful cook, a great hostess and she always looked amazing. But the fact that she also made her own evening dresses was something she liked to keep hidden for some reason. Father sometimes let it slip however! Mother was very beautiful and he was proud of her, but I remember they would be rowing about it when they came home. It wasn't the done thing at the time to have homemade evening clothes! But they were glorious dresses made of brocade, taffeta, silk and chiffon, and looked every inch haute couture. I can remember them to this day.

When our parents went out for the evening, they always came in to say goodnight before they left, Mother looking glamorous and Father often resplendent in his formal 'Mess' gear complete with cummerbund (which he sometimes let us wind around him!). We were left in the care of our Ayas. These women were all from Somalia, I'm not sure why, and sadly I don't recall an individual. But collectively I remember how beautiful the Somali women were, with their tall upright baring, their perfect haughty features and large eyes, their glowing skin and the exquisite fabrics they draped around themselves. They were gentle and kind but always slightly detached.

One day, Mark and I joined our parents in bed in the morning as was usual, and Father asked us if we knew what day it was. It was January 8th 1960, his birthday, and Mother had forgotten all about it! Her guilt must have been extreme and I assume we had no idea of dates. But when we headed out to Gold Mour for our usual afternoon swim, Father joined us and Mother presented him with a transistor radio, presumably she had gone shopping whilst we were at school. I think Father was pleased with that – both our parents loved listening to the radio.

It was in Aden that I first became aware of the volatility of our parents' relationship. They seemed to be going through a bad phase and I remember the tension and Mother's terse words that could conclude in a row, many of which became too explosive to ignore. I have a memory of Mark and me holed up in our bedroom hearing one such row being carried out at full volume through the walls of our parent's adjacent bedroom. We were standing side by side looking out of the window through the mosquito-netting casement and Mark turned to me, aged six, and asked if our parents were going to get divorced. I remember playing the adult and making comforting assurances that they were not. I hated the rows but I'm sure it never occurred to me that our family might not remain together as a result. And I don't think we were particularly perturbed. We were just waiting for it to be over, for the sun to shine from our mother again. And it wouldn't be long before our parents were being affectionate and laughing together once more. I think by now it had become the norm for us to see our parents swing between displays of anger and love. But there was no doubt that our parents had an unusual marriage.

I learnt many years later that there were times when my mother suspected Father of having been unfaithful to her. However proven or not proven Mother's suspicions were, her feelings of rejection, jealousy, resentment and loneliness when he was away were real and made her, in turn, vulnerable. She was very beautiful and attracted a great deal of attention wherever we were posted. But that is their story. And whatever phase their relationship was in at the time, the love and companionship our parents had for each other remained a constant, interspersed though it was with volatile and wordy arguments that no doubt chipped away at their marriage piece by piece, slowly eroding their relationship. It took twenty-five years to become too thin to sustain however, and throughout our childhood the four of us were, for the most part, an incredibly close-knit family with a strong sense of ourselves against the rest of the world, the 'mini tribe' that my brother called us.

At some stage during our time in Aden, Billie got divorced and it was decided that she should leave England for a while and come and join us. She duly arrived, got a job, bought a Fiat 500 that she named 'Depinto', joined our parent's social circle and created one of her own. We were very fond of our aunt and she fitted into our family well. Her presence made our mother happy and easier to please and there was a great deal of laughter in the house when Billie was around. And her 'difference' to Mother made her appear very sophisticated to us. She dressed in bolder colours than Mother did, with big jewellery, and she went to work every day. She also listened to jazz on the record player, much to our father's disgust. And embracing her new status as a single woman, Billie soon had one or two men friends in tow, and the occasional hurriedly ended conversations between Mother and Billie when we children put in an appearance added to the exotic mystery of her alternative lifestyle.

The family at Gold Mour

Billie seemed rather prone to drama however. I remember one morning soon after she arrived from England when Mother and Father had arranged a camel trip for her. Three customarily bad tempered camels arrived in our compound with their handlers and, after the prerequisite time it took to get them to lie down, Mother, Father and Billie duly climbed up into the saddles. But Billie squealed as the camel rose up with its jerky actions, a noise the camel presumably had never heard before and didn't like. The gates to the compound hadn't been closed properly and the camel saw its opportunity. It started to bolt towards them in a seemingly slow motion gallop across the compound and Billie's squeals increased in volume as it did so. In the event, the handler wasn't far away and was able to run to catch the trailing rope attached to the camel's nose peg. But it was a scary moment for Billie and I don't think she ever went on a camel again.

On another occasion, Billie had reason to collect us from school. She had been away for a few days and we were excited to see her. We climbed into the back of Depinto, always an awkward thing to do on account of the Fiat being so small. But as we headed home, there began to be a strong smell of burning and Billie eventually stopped the car by the side of the road and got out. Then she gave a little cry.

"Quick, children! Get out! I think the car's on fire!"

We struggled to clamber out to stand next to her on the road side and saw that flames and thick smoke were coming out of the engine, which was at the back of the car, just a few inches from where we'd been sitting! Billie had packed newspaper around the engine before she went away to protect it from sand and had forgotten to remove it before coming out to pick us up! We were lucky but I can't remember what happened to Depinto!

At some stage of our time in Aden I had an asthma attack, although I don't remember anything about it. But I was taken to hospital where the only memorable thing that happened, apart from being given a drug that helped my breathing but made my heartbeat very fast, was a visit from a friend of my parents, a young subaltern I think he was, who gave me a Bedouin brooch of a tiger claw set in brass with jewels all around. I suspect the jewels are glass, but I often wonder why he gave it to me and what its story is. Strangely, I was born in the Chinese year of the Tiger so consider it a talisman of sorts and I still have it. I never did like the idea of a tiger being killed to make it though, so I've never worn it. And after a week in hospital, I went home.

Intermittent asthma attacks became something that continued to trouble me throughout my childhood and the same drug always had the same alarming effect, making me feel very tired so that I had to stay in bed until the asthma passed. By the time I reached early adulthood, however, inhalers were prescribed which were far less debilitating and provided instant relief.

It's the end of a school day and Mark and I are looking forward to having lunch at Gold Mour. Mother is bringing a picnic today. We are very hot and can't wait to get into the sea, which we'll have to do before we eat our lunch as we aren't allowed to swim until an hour after we've eaten. Our parents are very strict about that.

I hold Mark's hand as we step into the harsh sunshine outside the entrance to the school. Mother is always parked outside, 'Isabella' making a splash of yellow against the sandy road. But today we can't see her and for a moment we stand confused as to what to do. Then we spot Billie running towards us.

"I'm collecting you today, children," she says with a quick smile. But she seems tense. And I wonder briefly why she isn't at work. We squeeze into the back of her little white Fiat with our bags on our knees.

"We're going straight home," she says, revving the car into a start and drowning out Mark's complaint. "Your mother has had a car accident."

She answers our questions as well as she can but she knows little except that Mother has been to the hospital but is now at home.

Billie drives erratically, sitting very close to the wheel and frequently grating the gears. Father says she isn't a very good driver. But we finally make it through the gates to the flats and run up the stairs. On opening our front door, the first thing we see is our large green food thermos, the one in which Mother puts our picnic lunches (a pasta or rice meal usually) all smashed up in the corner and covered in blood. Father comes out of their bedroom then, with his mouth set in a grim line, and he leads us in to see Mother. She is lying in bed, very pale and with a bandage around her head. She pulls herself up into a sitting position when we come in and opens her arms to hug us.

"Isn't this silly," she says as we go to her. "I'm fine, really."

Mother had been late for an appointment earlier in the day, maybe on account of making the pasta in tomato sauce that was to be our lunch. What she had been late for I never knew. But she took a hairpin bend too fast and the green thermos that she'd placed in the foot well of the passenger seat tipped over. She'd bent to right it in case the pasta sauce leaked out and then lost control of the car, which rolled twice, during which time she was thrown out of the windscreen, breaking the glass with her head. She had a dent in her head forever more after that.

Mother was obviously not fine. She was very shaken and bruised and had a bad headache for quite a while. And poor 'Isabella' was a right-off which upset her terribly. Then, soon after the accident, Mother developed pneumonia, a result of the shock the medical officer said. So the Army fitted air conditioning into our parent's bedroom, a huge box-like arrangement sitting outside the window that made a great deal of noise. It was thought the cooler air might help her breathe. In all the other rooms we had ceiling fans that whirred day and night but did little more than to stir the suffocating hot air around.

As Mother got better, it was decided that she needed to get away from the unhealthy air of Sheikh Othman and Aden. So she, Billie, Mark and I were sent to stay in Mukeiras, a small British garrison town situated high on an eight thousand foot plateau in the Protectorate state of Audhali, some hundred and twenty miles east of Aden near the North Yemen border, where the army had a lodge. We took one of the Arab bearers with us who would do our shopping and cooking, and we flew in a small plane with twin propellers. Father came to see us off.

As well as us, the plane contained a crowd of Arab tribes' people going home. They were laden with shopping and many had chickens and goats on their knees. The smell of the animals was very strong. The flight wasn't long however, and we landed safely on the dusty strip. And as the doors opened and we all climbed out, we felt the cooler fresher air straight away. Then the tribesmen on the ground began to welcome their family members back home by shooting live ammunition into the air.

"Stand under the wings, children," Mother said, "then you won't get shot!"

We stayed in the lodge, a small stone building that had a deep shady terrace and no electricity. We lit paraffin lamps at night and cooked on gas stoves, all of which added to the enchantment of the place and so different to Aden. The lodge was on the edge of what I remember as a leafy field with water running through it, where we had to walk carefully to avoid treading on a myriad of tiny frogs on the ground. It was a happy time and Mother slowly regained her health before we had to return to the desert heat of Aden.

Mother in Aden

Billie on a Dhow, Aden

Mark

'Stand under the wings, children' was foolish advice really but well-intentioned no doubt. The fuel tanks of the DC3 we flew in are in the wings and bullets that go up must come down!

We had a neighbour in Mukeiras, who lived across the field. I think he was an army vet. He showed my sister and me some strange things in hindsight. He had a very powerful microscope and pulled a hair from my head and showed me the follicle. Fascinating. He chopped the head off a chicken with an axe and we watched it run around headless for a while. My sister has long been vegetarian. You'd have to ask her!

Philippa and I loved having Billie around for many reasons, not least because she took parental focus off us. She never had her own children, so for the most part treated us as mildly annoying adults, which was refreshing. She was an accomplished painter and loved mainstream jazz. Until then we had been brought up on frequent dollops of Bach, the Brandenburg Concertos being a favourite, also Dvorjak and Tchaikovsky and all the greats, as well as Kathleen Ferrier, Paul Robson, and Burl Ives to name but a few. Our father hated the jazz but it was an interesting alternative.

Philippa

I doubt that Mark and I realised at the time that our childhood was in any way unusual. The other families we mixed with all had similar tales to tell. But later we could see it for what it was, a time of immense cultural stimulation, excitement and fun, with our parents at the helm.

Our father came in and out of our lives from his job of soldiering, exuberant and enthusiastic, but also impatient and challenging. He had an unquestioning sense of propriety and could easily lash out in anger if things went wrong. But his anger was always short-lived. He was basically a good humoured man, full of fun and laughter. He loved to whistle, and his songs rang out around the house whenever he was around.

He was also the centre of any social gathering, charming and amusing, a flirt with the ladies and generous to a fault in the officers' mess, despite the fact that money always seemed to be short. I remember this as a regular cause of bickering between our parents. We lived a privileged lifestyle thanks to the army, but unlike many of our parent's friends, we had no private means. Nor did we own a house in England. Everything we owned came with us around the world, carefully wrapped up in newspaper and loaded into huge wooden crates, the Heavy Luggage, that would then be shipped out to wherever we were going.

But it was our mother who was the centre of our universe and we adored her. A profoundly deep thinking woman with passionate opinions and a deep spiritual belief, she had a way with words that could make you want to follow her to the ends of the world, although the same eloquence and implacable stance could just as easily floor you in an argument! Affectionate, demonstrative and hugely sentimental, she always made us feel deeply loved. She had a wonderful irreverent sense of the ridiculous, able to reduce us all to tears of laughter with one look or one word and turn any happening into childish fun, often to our father's embarrassment. She was creative and artistic and encouraged us to be the same. She passed on to us her love of animals and nature. She read us all the childhood classics and brought them alive with different voices and silly faces. And she loved to sing. She had a beautiful singing voice. Both our parents loved music, and played their classical music at full volume on the 'Grundig' record player that followed us around the world. There was an abundance of joy in our family, but there were also tensions.

Mark and I recognised early on that our mother was a woman of contrasts. She could be wildly joyful, but she could just as easily be sad and moody for one reason or another and we grew up hating those times that took her away for a while. She also had a quick temper and when we made her angry, we were punished.

I clearly remember the punishments and the powerful sense of anger and powerlessness they instilled, but never the reason for them. And Mother was unbendable, refusing any further discussion after an incident, dismissing my feelings of resentment or being unjustly judged as 'sulking' and telling me to 'throw it away, Philippa', whilst changing the subject.

Whether these complexities of parenting were handled well or not is irrelevant. We were born in the 1950s when children had to behave or else and parents were permitted to get their own way! But whilst the duality to Mother's personality remained confusing to Mark and me for all her life, and her intractability sometimes caused discord between us, we learnt to accept it as the way things were. We absorbed the considerable love both our parents gave to us and learnt how to be angry in equal measures.

By the end of 1960, we were once again on the move. We were to go back to Barton Stacey in the UK where Father was to rejoin his regiment, the 25th Field Royal Artillery. And this time we flew. It was a night flight and I remember watching the propellers of the plane out of a window as lightning lit up the sky outside and the plane bucked and bumped through a storm. Somewhere towards the back of the packed plane, a baby cried and cried.

Our mother wrote about Aden in her later life:

'Do you remember the gardens in Sheikh Othman? Those high walls and iron gates? Once inside the stillness broken only by the chatter of birds and the sound of water splashing and spraying from the hoses, the shouts of the souk a distant echo? We'd walk there, you and I, early in the morning when the world was fresh and some of the coolness from the desert still lingered in the air.

'And sometimes in the evening, we'd go there to escape the airless end-of-day heat. There in the gardens was shade to be had under the oleander trees and the huge date palms. There was colour to feast our eyes on too; scarlet, pink, orange, yellow, purple and blue of orchids, iris, frangipani, oleander and camellias. The air was filled with their heavy perfume. There seemed nothing that wouldn't grow in that place. Sometimes we'd see a sudden rainbow caught in the shafts of sunlight and spray. How coarse the grass was, but so green all the year round. Such a balm for our eyes grown used to searching endless horizons in the desert that surrounded us.

'But oh, the desert, with its cruel heat and terrible sand storms, but also its magical sunrises and peace. Remember the way we used to ride out into it on the camels and watch as the sun broke over the horizon? Our eyes would catch mirages in the distance and sometimes a camel train would gradually materialise and pass us silently. First a donkey dwarfed by its shrouded rider. Then the heavily laden camels, their heads held high, their round feet plop plopping on the sand, the only other sound the jingle of harness and the murmur of the men as they passed. Their long journey was nearly over as they headed for Sheikh Othman, the last camel station. There they would be unloaded, rested and fed a while before heading back across the desert.

We meanwhile, would pass on in the coolness of the morning before turning for home.'

Sheikh Othman

Barton Stacey, England
(1960–1961)

Philippa

We lived in an army quarter on the Camp at Barton Stacey for three or four months and our time there was only made memorable by the arrival into our family of a Pekinese puppy we named Mouki. She was an adorable dog and became our mother's third 'baby', ruling the household and Mother's heart with a firm paw for over twelve years. As she grew up, and because of the little snorting noises she made when she was happy or asleep, she became known as Robinson after the Beatrix Potter character, Little Pig Robinson.

Mark and I got chicken pox. I went to the local forces' school, and presumably Mark did as well, where a rather creepy teacher with a large bushy moustache used to chase the girls at break time. And that's about all I can remember! Luckily, we weren't there for long and by the early spring of 1961, we were off to Germany with the regiment.

Mother and Mouki (Robinson)

Germany (1961-1963)

The 25th Field Regiment had been posted to Campbell Barracks in Hohne, central Germany, just outside the rather enchanting town of Celle. For this posting, Father was given command of one of the regiment's artillery units, 93 (Le Cateau) Battery,

The title 'Le Cateau' was awarded to the battery in 1961, both as a result of the battery's efforts in countering the Communist Terrorist Insurgency in Malaya in 1947, and because the battery had been famously instrumental in the defeat of the German Army in World War One at the Battle of Le Cateau in France. The battery then became known as 93 (Le Cateau) Battery and Father was always very proud to have been present at the award ceremony, which I believe took place in Le Cateau itself in northern France.

We moved into a large army quarter at the top end of a cul de sac where several other similar quarters lined both sides of the road, some bigger than others according to the rank of the occupant! In our garden was a large cherry tree that Mark and I were able to climb to pick the fruit, a lilac tree and many hedgehogs who lived around the periphery.

The house boasted a vast cellar divided into as many rooms as there were in the floor above. Here the boiler lived, into which Mother had to shovel coal on a regular basis. (After two years of doing this, she developed asthma from the coal dust). And here our huge wooden 'heavy luggage' crates were stored. When we came to pack up and leave two years later, a community of mice had taken them over, carefully shredding all the saved newspaper to make their nests. I remember the tiny pink babies that we had to relocate out into the garden.

Our time there passed busily and happily enough from my perspective. We travelled about a lot, guided by Father who was, as always, full of ideas and enthusiasm for the next adventure. And inevitably we took many photographs that help me remember, photographs that now included Robinson!

We walked in the Hartz Mountains; we visited Switzerland; we went to 'Shutzen Fests' (Fairgrounds) in Celle and 'Bier Fests' in Munich; we went to Frankfurt Zoo; and we took to canoeing on the river, the river Alle I think it was, Father and Mark in one Canoe, and Mother and I in the other, with the dog tucked in. And we visited Nuremburg and drove around the Nuremburg Ring in our family car, a much-loved black MG saloon! You could pay to do that and our parents were thrilled to put a dream into practice. We also took a memorable road trip over the border to East Germany and visited Berlin. We stood at the Brandenburg Gate which was cordoned off but we could see past the guards and over to the other side where grim looking buildings looked back at us.

We also got to know our maternal grandfather and his Czechoslovakian wife, Pim. Our grandfather was a rather cold and judgmental man of undoubtedly high intellect, but difficult to get close to. And Pim was confident and attractive but as equally quick to criticise as our grandfather! They were welcoming hosts however, and we visited them in their home in Karlsruhe and then further south in Aschau, in the mountains of Bavaria, where they had recently bought a picturebook house.

This was Heidi country, my favourite book at the time, and I fell in love with the house as soon as I saw it. It was a typical alpine house with carved wooden balconies and a steeply sloping double roof. The gardens went down to a stream, beyond which the fields were carpeted with wild flowers in the spring when we first saw it. I remember the clarity of the air and the silence, broken only by bird song and the sound of cow bells as the cattle grazed the lower slopes of the surrounding mountains. The bedrooms at the front of the house were built under the eaves of the roof and had sloping ceilings. And each had a balcony that looked out at the garden, the stream and the mountains. Here we were introduced to feather eiderdowns, the equivalent of modern duvets, and these would be thrown over the balconies in the mornings to air. And before we sat down to a breakfast of boiled eggs, black bread, Quark and honey, Pim would send Mark and me up the hill to the farm with a jug and a basket to collect warm milk straight from the cows and fresh eggs.

I always loved visiting them in Aschau despite the stresses of being made to feel inadequate! Pim was a wonderful cook and a superlative housewife, everything around her home being strictly and minutely managed. And these were all useful attributes as she and our grandfather successfully ran the house as a guesthouse for a while. Many years later, I was to spend a few weeks staying with them whilst studying for exams I subsequently never sat, after a change of heart about what I wanted to do when I left school! But it was a memorable and mostly enjoyable first foray away from home.

Back home in Celle, we had a pet hamster we named Herman, who Mother and Father would bring out when entertaining. He was a great success with their guests and would sit on the back of the sofa waiting to be given peanuts, which he would then stuff into the pouches in his cheeks to save for later. We got him a friend we named Claus. But where Herman was fat and cuddly, Claus was thin and mean and he'd bite you rather than let you play with him. And we learnt the hard way that you couldn't keep two male hamsters together anyway as they'd fight! So they had to have a cage each.

Mark and I also had pet mice called Pip and Squeak. We'd take them outside to play in the piles of grass after Father had mown the lawn. We didn't seem to be concerned about losing them. And we'd put each of them on one of our roller skates and give them a ride. Poor mice! They both died of cancer quite quickly.

When we had first arrived in Germany, Mark and I had gone to a local forces' school for children of all ages and all ability! It was incredibly rough but I don't think we were there long. All I remember about it were frequent and violent fights in the school playground between the 'big girls' who took off their stiletto heels to use as weapons against each other. I imagine our parents had been suitably horrified and I assume it was then that they cemented their decision to send Mark to boarding school in England. They considered him very impressionable and were concerned at his lack of interest in learning. He was seven!

Later, I went to a new forces' junior school and I have good memories of my friends, teachers and experiences there.

But not before my parents decided it would be a good idea for me to try out a German school in the area first. I spent a week there I think, before it was decided that a German school wasn't such a good idea after all. I can't remember why, although if I'd stayed there I would at least have been able to speak a language other than my own. My mother, Billie and their father and Pim all spoke German fluently, and although I could eventually understand more or less what was being said, it transpired that I am not gifted at learning languages!

As Mark turned eight, and the summer term came to a close, I remember the atmosphere at home being very stressful. Mark was going to boarding school in September and he often became angry and easily upset throughout that summer. Mother too was bad tempered a lot of the time and both our parents were intent on trying to make Mark 'knuckle down' and learn his times tables. They locked him in the study once, but he escaped out of the window and went to play with his friend next door, an act of such bravery and rebellion that had me terrified, shocked, and hugely admiring all at once. But the verbal backlash from our parents was extreme.

At the start of the September term, Mother accompanied Mark back to England to see him settled into his new school and then stayed a while with her family. After that first term, Mark flew back and forth for holidays on his own, together with all the other children from our social circle, each of them wearing a badge saying 'Unaccompanied Minor' on the plane.

I was alone amongst our peers in attending a local forces' school and was very envious of Mark's independence. As Mother would tell it, I didn't want to go to boarding school, which gives the impression that there was a choice. But the truth was that our parents only got financial help from the army for one child and would have found it difficult at that time to afford to send me as well. Maybe I was given a choice of some sort, I don't remember. I know Mother would have found it very hard to part with both her children and in any event, I doubt I would have wanted to leave her. I finally went to a private school as a day-girl for the last two years of my schooling, but that was after we'd moved back to England.

Grandfather's house in Aschau

Grandfather and Pim

On a walk

Mark

Germany was our next posting and we moved into 23 Memeleweg Strasse, Celle, an anodyne army quarter as I saw it, dumped with others like it outside the town of Celle. My sister and I were sent to school and for the life of me I can't remember a single thing about it. I had this friend who lived next door I think. He and I used to roam the wasteland at the end of the cul de sac with our air rifles, whether real or imaginary I've no idea. There were visits to my maternal grandfather on the Austrian border and a family holiday under canvas, neither remarkable from my perspective. I was bored and angry and didn't know why. My sister once spent some days building a house out of Lego, complete with stables, and

I kicked it to bits during an argument, subject unremembered. I have felt guilty about that ever since! Anyway, September 1961 arrived and my sister and I were forced to break our rather symbiotic relationship and go our separate ways.

Had I been eight in today's world, I would probably have been awarded some acronym based on my lack of concentration and I cannot say that I have anything but sorrow for anyone who has ever tried to teach me anything. The problem is that I have always fought authority even when it looks like a windmill, and I suspect that my mother, having tried to teach me herself, might have been very much looking forward to subcontracting my education to a nice middle class boarding school. I have no doubt that my parents were very concerned at my apparent lack of scholastic ability and I'm sure they thought they were doing the right thing.

Anyway, this form of education at the time was the norm amongst our extended tribe. The alternative would have been local schools or those attended by the children of 'Other Ranks' and thus losing one's place in the social order of things. There truly were no other options, especially if you were male. In those days, it was a given that the boy would be the eventual main earner in his future family. There was also an issue of cost. Then, as now, a private education did not come cheap and a boy's education was often given priority. It was only after my father left the army that I realised we had been able to live all those years both well and without financial concerns courtesy of Her Majesty.

Even so, I know that my parents struggled to pay my school fees sometimes. And I guess it was the main reason that my sister stayed at home and attended the forces' schools.

She was less influenced by external forces so didn't suffer educationally, although I believe she often felt socially marginalised, especially when I and all the other kids in our parent's social group returned for the holidays. This was perhaps redressed when we as a family returned to the UK in 1967 and she finished off her schooling at a Girls Public School in Guildford. I believe she hated every minute of that school however, marginalised again no doubt.

So I knew at this stage what my future held in store; expulsion from my mini tribe to prep school at Beech Hall, Macclesfield, Cheshire, England. A life sentence as I saw it then and still do. Build up the walls without, let the unformed malleable child writhe into a shape of sorts within, however many thrashings that require. It was the hardest thing I have ever undergone in my life to date and not of my choosing. Abandoned at this ghoulish place amongst people who didn't care for me in a country I barely knew nor actually wanted to. Tribeless.

Now I have met many a man in my travels who was subjected to the same treatment at similar ages, some as young as five, captains of industry, tramps, no matter what, and I and they will empathise and after a little while not need to refer to it again. We know that this type of behaviour towards children is a travesty, only made best of it by those with the strength of personality or muscle to crawl to the top of the heap, mostly at the expense of others. I can say, however, that throughout those years, I was never sexually abused. Only regularly beaten with canes and slippers, screamed at and made to feel less than human. As a result, I not so gradually developed disrespect for anyone or any institution that sought to control me either educationally or sort to harm me physically.

I liked reading almost anything and found pretty much everything else boring. As previously mentioned, an holistic peek at my lack of educational accomplishments would have revealed a possible solution to my problems or at least whether there was one. I have apparently a high IQ! This alone should have alerted these faux educationalists who were charging my parents a fortune to find a path through for this clearly troubled child who was lurking in the bottom third of his class, with the exception of English, for five years at their so called Centre of Excellence. In truth, they didn't give a shit and consequently neither did I. Just Bad Reports, Could Try Harder, Send Another Check.

Gosh, this is cathartic! It disturbs me still this far down the line. Well, it could all have been so much worse or so much better. My point, I suppose, is that young children are fragile, malleable and brimming with hope, and in most cases talent in one form or another. And it takes vocational talent to encourage and bring them on, not threats of violence and punishment. I hope things have changed, and I don't doubt that there are prep schools up and down the land which the pupils adore attending.

Beech Hall at that time however was owned and run by a Mr Hunt and his wife who acted as de facto headmaster and assistant headmaster. There were no girls at that time. The Hunts' daughter and son in law, Worthington by name, were the next level of command. The remaining staff, who seemed all to me to be ancient, confined their teaching skills, such as they were, to reading textbooks aloud. They chose their favourite pupils early on and installed them in a purpose built dorm where no one ever got beaten. Us lesser kids for example, had we presented a messy trunk or not done a proper hospital corner, would be taken outside the dormitory door and given 'six of the best' with the heal of our slipper. The command 'outside the dorm' still pisses me off. It hurt and is not conducive to a good night's sleep. I begged my mother to send moccasin type slippers but they actually hurt worse.

I had a safety net during my time at Beech Hall in the guise of my aunt, my mother's sister, Joan, and her family who lived an hour's drive away, as well as my maternal grandmother who lived nearby. Both my cousins were pupils at Beech Hall so I often spent two or three of our allowed exeat weekends with them. Joan was a woman I liked enormously. She was rather fay and clearly bored with the 1960s drudgery of being a 'Stepford Wife' type housewife of the day. Her method of transport was a Bond Bubble car that required kick starting. She was an elegant woman and I have an enduring memory of her, a Kensitas cigarette in mouth, swearing at this engine that was always reluctant to start and inevitably laddered her stockings.

My cousins Mike and William were also at Beech Hall but we didn't see much of each other. Michael, because he was a stratospheric two and a half years older and a member of the 'Chosen Few', and William, because he and I joined different tribes who only randomly met.

John, Joan's husband, was an outdoors sort of chap and into shooting birds and fishing for trout. They had a 1930s second class sleeper railway carriage planted in a beautiful valley in Wales with a small hut and a vegetable garden. We would spend weekends there shooting pigeon with a 12 bore, a bruised shoulder for an eight year old but great fun. And I learnt to tickle trout and catch them with worms. We ate and prepared everything we killed. It was straight out of Huckleberry Finn and a smooth bit on the learning curve of growing up. Lessons learnt in the field so to speak are of so much more use than dust ingested from creaky books in many respects.

Mark at Beach Hall

Philippa

I can't remember how much I missed Mark when he left. My memory has blanked it. I presume as a child one accepts the status quo. But I suppose our mother, a central force in our lives, was a conduit for the relationship Mark and I had at the time, a relationship that had obviously always included her. So after Mark left, my main focus turned on Mother and I began to feel a growing responsibility for her wellbeing. We were very close and she was not always very happy in those days. Whatever else was going on in her life at the time, she missed Mark dreadfully. And she must have felt such pain every time he left. But with no other resource to nurture Mark's educational needs as our parents saw it, she must have felt restricted to adhering to the tribal patterns of 'our sort'. Mark wrote so many heartbreakingly beseeching letters to Mother from school however, in such childish writing, that reading them as an adult and a mother myself, I don't know how she could have borne it. I'm not sure she did very well. She kept every one of those letters all her life and felt a huge guilt.

During the winter of 1961/2, shortly after Mark had left, there was a vast amount of snow and Father took his troops to the mountains to learn to ski, winter combat training I suppose it was. To cheer Mother up, it was suggested that she and I (and Robinson) should tag along and we all duly stayed in a tiny very primitive cabin in the mountains. Mother and I never did learn to ski properly, but we had a lot of fun in the snow and it was lovely to see her happy. We put the dog on a sledge every morning and walked down to the little town through the deep snow to collect provisions, then trudged back up the mountain again to the cabin.

There was no doubt that Mark being sent away to school changed the dynamic of our family. When he came home for holidays, Mark and Mother were as they always had been, a small boy and his mother linked in physical togetherness and

121

love. But both our parents, consciously or unconsciously, were so intent on making sure Mark had a good time that it would all feel a bit staged sometimes.

Mark and I quickly clicked back into our normal relationship however, and we had as much fun together as we always had. If I was at all aware of the homesickness and distress he was going through at the time, I didn't question it. I assumed it was a rite of passage with no alternative other than to accept the situation as it was. I truly felt he was the privaledged one. When he came home for holidays, he always put on a brave face with me, full of bravado and stories of his antics at school and he seemed happy enough. But his school experiences seemed another world away to me. And as we grew up, the alienating differences in our life experiences increased and would eventually lead us down very different paths, but we would remain close if not always in tune.

It was apparent early on that Mark had turned to music as a protection against his homesickness. He'd come home full of the latest songs that he and his friends had been listening to and I felt increasingly very left 'behind the times' as I didn't know any of them! It was a few years before I became interested in the 'cultural revolution' of the early 60s, and by 1962/3, the most 'modern' I had become was when Mother and I tried to learn the 'Twist' to the radio, with great hilarity. But Father had come in to the room and seen us and been horrified at our actions. I have to admit that the Twist was never a particularly attractive dance and must have looked abhorrent to my father who was a wonderful ballroom dancer.

For Mark, however, this time was the beginning of a lifelong passion for the music and philosophies of the future legends and poets of the 60s, and his love of their music and a need to question the status quo was something that continued all his life.

I now know that our parent's relationship had reached some sort of crisis point at that time. I don't remember details, although I remember Mother going back to England a few times over that last year in Germany, or at least being away. Her sister, Joan, was going through some emotional problems and I suppose she would have visited Mark at the same time. Robinson and I and the rodents were left with friends, or with Father if he was at home. although he too was away on army exercise a lot of the time.

Meanwhile, I started piano lessons with a very strict German teacher who had little patience with the fact that once I had heard a piece played on the piano, I would try to play by ear rather than learn to read the music.

I also discovered horses! I think my parents had done their best to make sure my life was filled so that I wouldn't miss Mark too much, and they had got me a weekend job helping to muck out at the army stables. There's a photograph in the Germany album of me reaching up to cuddle a huge horse called Kilcorn, who was my favourite among the horses in the stables. Mucking out was hard work, but for me it was the beginning of a long love affair with horses, something I shared with my mother when we were posted out to Malta in 1963.

Once again we were on the move. Having received our marching orders, Mother and I clicked into a well-rehearsed course of action. We started to pack! The wooden crates were heaved up from the cellar (minus the mice and with the able help of Father's batman) and everything apart from what we immediately needed in our new home was carefully wrapped in newspaper and packed, heavy items first, lighter more fragile items on top.

We also had to check the house inventory of things the army had provided and make a list of anything that had been broken; holes in the walls where we'd hung pictures had to be plugged up (Mother and I perfected the art of doing this with toothpaste!) and the house had to be cleaned, we and our Putzfrau (cleaning lady) all working together. Finally the quatermaster would visit and, if we 'passed muster', all would be cleared for our departure.

It was decided that Mother and I would drive to Malta, whilst Father went on ahead. But first Mother drove the MG back to England to replace it with something bigger, and to collect Billie, who was to accompany us on the trip. She returned to Germany in a large cream coloured Station Wagon (make and model unremembered!) and in October 1963, Mother, Billie and I set off with the dog to drive to Malta. I was two months short of thirteen and Mother and Billie were two months short of thirty-five. We were all December-born Sagittarians!

Malta (1963-1966)

We have a tent, a primus stove, a few army mess tins to cook in, a small aluminium kettle and a washing up bowl. Also a box of provisions; tea, coffee, powdered milk, cereal, baked beans, sardines, etc. All this is packed into the back of the Station Wagon. We buy anything else we need on the way. We have a map of Europe with campsites and Agip petrol stations marked on it.

The Agip petrol stations are easy to spot on the road as they display a huge sign of a dragon breathing out fire and we discover that these are lit up at night. Mother is proud of her map reading skills. But as she is the driver, Billy sits next to her and does her best to follow the route she and Mother work out the evening before. I sit in the back with Robinson.

There are virtually no other English cars on the roads and this, together with the voiced concerns of so many family and friends echoing in our ears, makes our journey feel like a huge adventure!

"Three females, all on your own, all the way to Malta!"

"What if you get a puncture?"

"What if you break down?"

"What about the Mafia in Sicily?"

All these comments had made Mother even more determined to undertake the drive however. Nothing phases her it seems. Besides, we have each other and we feel invincible.

Our first stop is to stay overnight with my grandfather and Pim in Karlsruhe, so setting off from them the next morning feels like the proper start to the journey and we are all in high spirits. Mother and Billy are so funny together that sometimes my sides hurt from laughing so much. This does help the many hours we spend in the car to pass. But we aren't in too much of a rush and there's so much to see on the way.

We stop for picnic lunches or to get petrol or provisions and to let the dog stretch her legs. There's often a bit of difficulty finding the camp site we are aiming for but once we do so and stop for the night, we put up the tent, unload our sleeping bags, blow up the lilos and settle down to cooking a meal on the stove.

The tent is only meant for two, so we have to sleep very close together in a row. Robinson has the area at the top of the tent with the bags. At night, our lilos seem to take turns in deflating and the noise the foot pump makes as we blow them up again induces much muffled hysterical laughter from Mother and Billie. In the morning, we pack it all up again and load it into the back of the Station Wagon. As the days go on, we get more and more proficient at making and breaking camp and loading and unloading the car, and we feel very proud of our skills.

We stop off in Bologne and drift around the piazzas to soak up the Italian atmosphere. Billy speaks a bit of Italian but it seems to consist mostly of hand movements. Then we visit Lake Garda for a walk around before heading south to Florence. Here, we camp in an olive grove near Fiesole in the hills above Florence and watch the sun set over the city. The next day, I have my first sighting of the beautiful Ponte Vecchio in Florence as we walk beside the Arno.

From Florence, we continue south. We bypass Rome and get lost in Naples, the lines of washing hanging above every street confusing our sense of direction. We come out eventually and head for Pompeii, although it's closed when we get there. There's a small museum that's open and we visit that instead. It's rather grim so we drive on towards Sorrento for the night.

Mother and Billie want us to drive along the Amalfi coast road the next day. But first we camp by the sea. It's hot and dry and we are told that the campsite has an infestation of ants, but that if we camp lower down nearer the water there shouldn't be so many. We have to unload the car and carry everything down to the lower area, and after putting up the tent amongst the wonderful smelling pine trees, we sit for a while exhausted. We watch as a young man comes out of the sea and walks towards us, shaking the water from his hair and face like a dog. He is dressed only in a pair of tight black bathing trunks and is very tanned.

"Buonasera," he says, smiling, then goes into the next tent and we hear the zip close.

Billy and Mother exchange a look and Billy pats her hair and rummages around in her bag for some lipstick. The man is gone for some time but eventually we hear the zip of his tent once again and we all turn. But he is not as he was, half naked and wet. The man is a priest and is dressed accordingly. He smiles at us again and walks away with purpose. Once he's out of hearing, Mother and Billie collapse with laughter.

The Amalfi coast road is extraordinary. Tiny roads wind precariously around the steep cliffs then drop down to fishing villages where the houses seem to be perched one above the other up the slopes. We stop in Positano for lunch. Then we carry on south, stopping to look around the ruins of the Greek Temple at Paestum.

Then we head into the toe of Italy, a place where few English people go and definitely not women on their own. I sense Mother and Billie's growing tension. They decide we need to treat ourselves to a night in a motel. We need a good wash at the very least.

It's quite late when we see the lit-up sign for a motel on the road and we stop. We all get out of the car to go into the motel and Billie begins to speak with the manager who looks at us suspiciously whilst backing away from Billie as she speaks. Billie persists but seems to take a while to make herself understood. Suddenly, Mother realises what the problem could be and tells Billie quietly in English that her waving hands must smell of the sardines we ate at lunchtime! By the time we are shown to an upstairs room, we are all helpless with laughter and the motel manager has made a hasty retreat.

The car ferry from Italy to Sicily only takes half an hour and we then head south. The countryside is barren and deserted. Suddenly Mother looks concerned and pulls up on the side of road. We have a puncture. Mother and Billy begin to empty the back of the Station Wagon to get at the spare wheel and tools whilst I walk Robinson up and down a bit, but it's very warm. Then we notice the dust of a car approaching.

Mother and Billy look at each other and I see Mother take a knife out of the camping box. We stand there as the car comes nearer. A single man is driving and he slows. I think of the tales of the Mafia in Sicily and the dangers of women travelling alone. The man stops his car and gets out. He looks at our wheel and says something in Italian, and we realise he is offering help. He makes changing the wheel look easy and is very charming as he accepts our thanks and continues on his way.

Finally we arrive at the ferry terminal and make ready to board the overnight ferry to Malta. Mother has become more and more silent and stressed. She must be very tired, but her main fear is that she will have to part with Robinson once we dock in Valletta. Malta has strict quarantine rules, especially as we have come from Germany that doesn't.

We are given a dark cabin in the bowels of the old ferry. Piping and wiring that pass through the cabin were once painted yellow but they, like the rest of the cabin, are now thick with dirt and dust. The single blanket on each of the bunks is stiff and scratchy and there is a strong smell of oil. A single tiny porthole sits just above the water level.

The toilet outside the cabin is seemingly next to the ships engines and the noise once we get under way is almost unbearable. Robinson is terrified. She pants and shivers and tries to run away, but there's nowhere to go. Mother does her best to calm her and the night passes, but none of us sleep. The crossing is very rough and Mother's distress and Robinson's terror are catching. I feel sick much of the time and am thankful to see the sky lighten and know we are nearly there.

We sail into Valletta and get a brief glimpse of honey coloured stone walls and battlements before we go down to the car deck and wait to dock. Mother loads Robinson into her shopping basket and secures the basket clasp at the top, but her grim face tells me not to ask. We get into the car and drive off the ferry onto the docks and join a queue of cars, lorries and people. There's a lot of shouting and everything seems very disorganised.

Suddenly we see Father striding towards us and it's such a relief to see him. With him is a short Maltese man who Father introduces as his driver, Paul. Mother's eyes, meanwhile, tell Father everything he already knows about the dog and he immediately takes charge! He takes the basket from Mother and gives it to Paul.

"Please come with me, Mrs Hilpern," Paul says to her with confidence.

Father nods. So we follow Paul on foot, past the line of waiting cars, towards a group of uniformed customs officials. Paul greets them in Maltese and tells them with some authority who we are. They look towards Father who is now driving our car in the queue, and then towards his waiting army Landrover. They hold their hands out for our passports. Mother has her imposing expression in place, which is assertive and not to be argued with. She looks every inch a British Army officer's wife! They glance at her and at the passports. Then they wave us on. We walk to where the Landrover is parked and Paul opens the doors for us to get in. Then he places the basket with Robinson in gently beside Mother. She grasps his hand.

"I can't thank you enough," she says, choking back a sob.

Paul gives us a wide smile and winks. Then we all look at each other and, as Mother wipes her eyes, we can't stop grinning. Robinson is free, Mother is happy again and we all feel totally euphoric as we drive out of the docks and into the glorious Maltese morning.

Mother, Billie and me in Malta

Mark

During my early expulsion from our small tribe, the family moved to Malta. My mother, sister and Billie drove from Germany chiefly in order to facilitate my mother's Pekingese to be smuggled into the country. The Hilpern luck in securing excellent quarters had returned and we were billeted in the top half of a medieval tower, Torri Cumbo. A very fine house with acres of cool tiled floors, ceilings as high as a church and walls so thick that coolness and warmth were guaranteed year round. We spent three years there and where, from my perspective when allowed out of my prison in Cheshire, we all had a fabulous posting in our own way.

My father's job was to assist with the public relations engendered around the forthcoming Independence of Malta from the British Empire in 1964. I still have no idea why he was chosen for such a job, but as a family we enjoyed being there enormously. My sister lucked out again and attended the forces' school on the island where I believe she was happy enough and did well.

My parents had a rather manic social life and my mother made her own friends and learnt how to ride horses. Also, it should be said, I took baby steps in learning how to flirt with my sister's friends and developed a crush on one of them, Ann Richards. We wrote to each other from our respective prisons 'back home', she from a convent in the Isle of Wight.

Holidays in Malta were great fun and probably the happiest time of my childhood. We walked and swam and rode and I enjoyed the rationed company of my family enormously. I could drop the rebel stance for a while. So many small memories; like lying on my mother's bed watching her back comb her hair then putting it into a bun, and the ubiquitous head scarf and Joy perfume to finish; and my father being wound into his cummerbund prior to another skip down the road of their seemingly endless social life.

We spent our weekends on a launch diving and swimming off the small island of Comino, or we stayed on the island of

Gozo, always punctuated by route marches around the island with my father striding on ahead with pipe in mouth and walking stick in hand. Philippa and my mother would chatter along behind him with the illegal immigrant dog whilst I would more often than not be bringing up the rear clutching my air rifle. I wasn't so keen on walking!

During this posting, my father took to reading to us en famille, either whilst we sat on the rocks by the sea after a picnic lunch, or at home in the drawing room before bedtime. I mostly remember the *Captain Blood* series of novels by Rafael Sabatini. Stirring stuff and in its own way made me feel part of the family again. And my sister and I invented two alter egos, Caroline and Oswold, based I think on an amalgam of junior army officers and their wives who we had met over the years. At the end of every school holidays, our parents would invite us to dinner in that guise and we would dress up in grown up clothes and be given watered down wine.

In the summer of 1962, the Moors Murderers, Bradey and Hindley, were caught and the horror of their crimes saw light of day. In Malta, we received English newspapers and I remember flicking through the Sunday Express and coming across two pages stapled together. It transpired that my mother, wishing to save my sister and me from the evils being uncovered in the court case, deemed it necessary to sensor and protect us from them. My sister seemed happy with the status quo at the time, however I was unable to live with those staples remaining in place and had to read every word that was on offer. I was, of course, appalled. Even brought up on a diet of Holocaust, even having visited Belsen whilst we were in Germany, this was contemporary and an open festering wound in our society that seemed unthinkable and specifically that children were involved. I'm not sure how this affected me as a nine year old. Another dollop of adult mistrust in all likelihood.

When the eve of my departure arrived, I was allowed to choose my 'last supper', usually braised kidneys in red wine, rice and peas. I would buy my mother a present prior to my departure, habitually a Pyrex dish for some reason or other. I hated leaving and arriving back at Beech Hall.

Much has been written about how the passage of time during one's youth appears to pass so much slower than in later years, but I can't remember the science behind it. Something to do with brain growth and perhaps nascent experiences having a greater impact on the psyche. School, as does prison I suppose, took on a patina of normality. I made no close friends, read a lot and did not excel at anything. I was a slightly below average student in everything bar English Literature, Language and bizarrely French. I found sports pointless and did most things I could not to conform. As I remember though, I was not desperately brave and always did just enough to be retained within the meniscus of conformity. I exceeded briefly as a choirboy. I had perfect pitch but not much substance to my voice, enough however to be singled out for the odd soprano solo. I think that I soaked up the accolades for a while and then felt that such feelings were a sell out to the powers that be, a nascent rebel without a proverbial cause.

My time at Beech Hall ground on remorselessly towards the Common Entrance exam. And I continued to be a poor student. In todays educational system, I believe I would have been diagnosed as a member of the Attention Deficit Disorder tribe and, at a decent educational facility, would have been treated and taught accordingly rather than being regularly beaten, which in my case clearly produced merely negative results. But this was 1963.

I'm sitting in the wheelhouse of my Dutch barge on the Thames writing this, staring down the thick end of the telescope of time fifty years on and can't recall a single event during that last year at prep school worth recording. I look myopically at these Lowryesque figures and try to flesh them out occasionally without much success.

Torri Cumbo – our house in Malta

Philippa

I believe our parents had made a 'make or break' truce before going to Malta. Their relationship in Germany had seen some hard times, but whatever the reason, something had been sorted and concluded, and I think they saw the move to Malta as a new beginning for them. And the three years we spent on the island would turn out to be the happiest for us all.

Surrounded by a sea of the clearest blues, Malta will always be golden in my mind, as it was on the morning we arrived. It was actually very green in the winter when the rains came storming in, and resplendent in the spring with glorious wild flowers in every meadow and along every secret valley. We used to pick bunches of wild Narcissi and send them in boxes to my grandmother in England.

But when we arrived in early autumn, the crops had been harvested and the ground was dry and rocky, the iconic low walls of local honey coloured stone crisscrossing the land to show the demarcation of fields. The same golden stone was used to build all the houses, from the many gracious villas set deep inside their leafy gardens to every single church (of which there were many) down to the humblest single story dwellings. The land shimmered gold in the sun that day and our enchantment with Malta began as Paul gave us a brief guided tour on the way to our new home just outside the village of Mosta.

Mosta was then a small bustling town in the centre of the island famous for its huge circular cathedral topped by one of the largest unsupported domes of its kind. The cathedral stands tall in the town's central square with steep wide steps leading up to its doors, its position affirming the placement of religion in the Maltese community. The bells of Mosta Dome called worshippers to pray, take Mass or make their confessions many times a day. And when the priests walked around the town, people stopped to genuflect and cross themselves as they passed by. Some would be brave enough to approach the priests and kiss their rings. In this devoutly Roman Catholic country, where religion governed all aspects of life, priests were the Fathers of the flock and to be revered.

We discovered in time that every town in Malta had a Saints day, when the huge and heavy religious statues, that normally resided in the churches, were placed on pallets and carried out on the shoulders of a dozen strong men. The statues were then paraded around the town amidst great religious fervour and a mildly hysterical carnival atmosphere. The biggest processions took place all around the island on Good Friday, when the statues were accompanied by those who felt they needed to do penance, some by carrying life-sized crucifixes and others who stripped off and whipped themselves raw as they processed.

The centre of Mosta was noisy. Cars used their horns freely and buses waiting in the square with their engines running filled the surrounding air with diesel fumes. Traders with horse or donkey carts laden high with merchandise whipped their animals to go faster whilst shouting out whatever it was they were selling. And occasionally, a frothing high stepping 'trotting' pony pulled its two-wheeled race cart through the town at high speed. We learnt that this harness racing is a Maltese passion as dangerous as any motor-bike to both horse and rider.

Driving down one of the narrow side streets leading out of the square, small shops opened out onto the streets, their entrances dark against the glare. On the pavements outside, groups of men were seated on chairs and they stared at us as we passed. In many of the doorways, women sat making lace, chatting all the while, their usage of the pegs and cotton threads incomprehensible to any but themselves. Some of the older women wore the extraordinary Maltese national costume of a huge black cloak with a stiffened canopy over their heads. And all along the street, suspended high up, were tiny cages of captured birds who were singing into the hot sky. It was a strong tradition, we were soon to learn, to hunt wild birds during the migration season by using trapped ones as decoys.

Later, as we explored the island, we would find shooting hides when walking on the cliffs, from where the hunters would indiscriminately shoot birds as they flew in across the sea during the 'season'. I believe at the time of writing that this practice still goes on despite multinational criticism and a global recognition of the need to protect migrating birds. There is no place in our challenged modern world for this so called 'sport'. I don't believe the birds are even eaten but I may be wrong.

Leaving the town, small flat roofed dwellings had sacking hanging over their doorways and evidence of a living scraped out of the dust around each. Most had chickens and a tethered goat or two behind the house, and many had a dog tied up on the roof. The sound of a distressed dog barking was to become a deeply held emotional trigger that can transport me back to Malta at any time. Mother and I would later convince the local smallholders to at least give these animals water if not shade in the heat of the day.

The apparent inhumanity towards animals and wildlife in Malta at that time was something we never came to terms with. But it seemed to come from inherited ignorance rather than innate cruelty. We once apprehended a man beating a horse in the shafts of his cart. Mother leapt from our car and shouted at the man to stop. He turned around looking shocked at this interference.

"But he bit me," was his reply, childlike in its simplicity and difficult to reason with.

The lane out of Mosta continued eventually along a high wall, behind which our new home, Torrie Cumbo, towered above its enclosed gardens and, with its 360 degree view, stared back at Mosta Dome on one side and the ancient hill top town of Medina on the other.

Torri Cumbo was impressive. We never lost that sense of wonder that it had become our home and we loved it from the moment we first set eyes on it. We entered through vast wrought iron gates, framed by palm trees, into an outer garden, then on through another gateway into the main courtyard. Beyond this was a further walled garden boasting a fountain and rows of orange and lemon trees.

Built from the traditional honey coloured stone, the five storey tower itself had been divided into two halves to provide two separate living areas. We had been given the top three floors of the building, accessed from the courtyard by wide stone steps that wound around a central open turret and onto a higher terrace. Once a sentry post, the central turret housed a huge aviary of budgerigars!

Inside our home wide stone staircases, that dipped in the middle from five hundred years of use, connected us to our three levels and the flat roof. The main living area was on the central level, where each room had tiled floors, lofty ceilings and floor to ceiling windows. These all opened like doors onto a wrought iron balcony that wrapped around the house, an arrangement that was to lead to great games of hide and seek, where it was only silence and stealth that won you the game.

In the bottom half of the building lived a WRAC Officer, Major Alma Crofton, who became a great family friend, and across the courtyard in what had been the coach house lived another army family by the name of Goodridge. I believe he was an army dentist.

I realise now how incredibly privileged we were to live in what has since become a national monument. Torri Cumbo (or Cumbo Tower) was a privately owned medieval tower that had, in the 16th century, served as a stronghold against attack from Turks and Moors. More recently, it had been used as an RAF Officers' Mess during World War Two, and presumably during the 1960s when we were in Malta, it had been rented from the owner for army officer accommodation. But Torri Cumbo was most famously known locally as the subject of a sung legend handed down from the Middle Ages known as the *Bride of Mosta*.

It's very long but essentially tells the story of a Count and his family who lived in Torri Cumbo with their beautiful daughter, Marianne. One of their servants was a captured Turk, Haggi, who fell in love with Marianne and, when given his freedom, decided to kidnap her and take her back to Turkey where he was a sultan. This he did, on the eve of Marianne's wedding to her beloved, Toni, fatally stabbing Marianne's father in the process. With Marianne then a prisoner in the sultan's palace, Toni sailed for Turkey to find her. Once he'd done so, Marianne persuaded a maid to help them escape and she and Toni sailed back to Malta and were married!

Malta is an island steeped in stories and history and there were, and still are, plenty of Neolithic dwellings, Megalithic temples and vast perfectly preserved underground catacombs to visit, evidence of the island's prehistoric occupation. Later in history, the island was colonised in turn by the Phoenicians, the Romans, the Byzantines and the Arabs before being invaded by the Normans and becoming Christian, and the impact of centuries of attack, siege, occupation and government have all left their stamp on the architecture and the people of the island.

Much of Malta's more modern influence dates from the early Middle Ages, when the islands were occupied and subsequently ruled over for nearly three hundred years by the Knights of St John, a Roman Catholic military order associated with caring for pilgrims returning from the holy land. Their symbol of an eight pointed cross is still the emblem of Malta today.

In the early 16th century, increasing conflict between the Ottoman Empire and the Christian West meant that Malta, as a place of strategic importance in the Mediterranean, was often under attack by the Turks. To counter this, the knights built the massive fortressed walls of the Grand Harbour, fortifications that eventually proved pivotal in their success in staving off Turkish occupation.

At the same time Malta, together with many parts of Christian Europe, was enduring the prolonged period of harsh religious Inquisition, where individuals could be persecuted for anything that could be seen as being in support of heresy or Protestantism. The system of tribunals, torture and condemnations was finally overruled when the island was briefly occupied by Napoleon in 1798, after which time the Inquisitors fled, deserting their fine palaces and prisons.

We would visit these crumbling buildings and climb amongst the ruins, and I was deeply affected as a young teenager by their silent testimony to over two hundred years of religious tyranny. Napoleon, meanwhile, after being defeated by Lord Nelson in Alexandria, finally handed Malta to the British in 1813, in whose hands it remained until Independence in 1964.

During the First World War, Malta became known as the 'Nurse of the Mediterranean' on account of the hundreds of thousands of wounded allied troops taken to the island after heavy fighting in Gallipolli. But it was Malta's role in World War Two that earned the island its greatest accolade.

Seeing the allies using Malta as a valuable refuelling post, German and Italian forces began to attack the island in 1940. Malta went on to endure two gruelling years of intensive and constant bombing, and in a bid to starve the population into surrender, any allied ship trying to take aid to the island was also bombed.

Ultimately, the defence put up by the British RAF and Royal Navy ensured that by the end of the two years much of the German and Italian fleets were destroyed without a landing ever made. And in November 1942, a convoy of allied forces finally made it through to the Grand Harbour in Valetta, bringing much needed supplies. Soon afterwards, the German and Italian forces withdrew from their efforts to capture the island and King George presented the people of

Malta with the George Cross, in honour of their resilience and courage, an award that is still depicted on the national flag today.

Father's new role was as public relations officer, presumably working at promoting the role of the British Army in Malta at a time of great change, as the island headed towards its forthcoming independence. He was based in the offices of the very grand Castille Palace in the centre of Valletta and, apart from a brief stint in Cyprus with the United Nations Peacekeeping Forces, he was in this role for nearly three years.

He had a delightful group of Maltese office staff, all of whom became friends, including a secretary called Maria Bussutil. When Maria heard that I was taking piano lessons, and we didn't have a piano for me to practice on, she insisted that I practice at her parent's home on theirs. So, for the three years we were in Malta, I went to the Busuttil's house once a week after school.

Mr and Mrs Bussutil were small round people who were incredibly warm and welcoming. Their home was filled with religious treasures and potted plants and all the chairs were draped with Maltese lace antimacassars. When I arrived there from school, always hungry, they would make me Hobz Biz Zejt, which translated means bread with oil, a Maltese open sandwich made with thick slices of the traditional bread called Hobza, a type of sourdough, liberally spread with mashed tomato, drizzled with oil and sprinkled with mint, capers, olives and salt. I could never eat enough of them!

Considerable worth was given to food in Malta. During our time there, Maria got married and I remember us crowding around her parents' dining table admiring all her wedding gifts, the pride of which was a huge pasta machine that spewed out all shapes of pasta when you filled it with dough.

My school, Tal Handaq, was a Royal Naval Comprehensive Co-educational school for British forces' children in Malta. Paul would pick Father and me up from Torri Cumbo in the mornings in the Landrover, and I would be dropped off in Mosta to catch the school bus. But if we were late, I had to endure the toe curling embarrassment of having Father's driver follow the bus to the next stop, our presence causing much hilarity with the cool kids who sat in the back of the bus. As I was one of very few officer's kids at the school, I hated to be seen as elitist in any way.

We were bused in from all corners of the island, the vehicles old even in those days, spewing out their fumes and jostling for places in the parking area at the school. I remember being daunted by the sheer number of them, and by the timetable, and the logistics of getting around such a vast area where double storey classrooms and modified Nissan huts taught over twelve hundred pupils. But it soon became normality and I can honestly say that Tal Handaq was the only school that I have more good memories of than bad! The sports facilities and playing fields were impressive, the number of subjects offered was vast, and I believe the education was of the highest standard, although as a school for children of all abilities, it was by no means without its rougher elements.

I found myself behind in the Sciences and Maths, something that remained a constant throughout my formal education. And I found Latin and French hard, all attempts to learn any language remaining futile my whole life! But I was always in the top stream for English, History and the Arts and those were my passions.

I made some good friends over the three years we were there and, as my teenage years advanced, I had crushes on several of the boys and had a few 'dates' with some! I also learnt to take boys with a pinch of salt, the benefit I believe of co-education. But that's an argument for another time!

Sports days came and went and I discovered I could run quite well for short distances and jump quite a long way in the long jump. Using the gymnasium apparatus terrified me, but I grew to love the trampoline. I had a very minor part in a school production of Gilbert and Sullivan's *The Pirates of Penzance* wearing a skirt made of crepe paper. And I took part in a school fashion show in my final year, I and my fifteen year old friends modelling the clothes we had made in sewing class.

There were other cultural treats on offer in Malta. We once went to watch Swan Lake performed by a German ballet company, although my main memory of that performance was of one of the dancers in the chorus line who forgot to take off her brightly coloured leg warmers and had to pirouette her way off stage to remove them. This, and the dust that rose from the old stage as the dancers performed, set Mother off into such contagious hysterical laughter that we both had to leave the theatre!

But more memorable were the visits to Malta by an Italian Opera Company who performed at the Royal Opera House in Valletta. This was an annual highlight. We'd dress up for the occasion and sit in the best seats to watch Madame Butterfly, La Boheme, Carmen and The Magic Flute, and I fell in love with opera. For my 14th birthday, my parents bought me the single record of Maria Callas singing Un Bel Di from Madame Butterfly. I was, and still am, unable to hear it without crying.

Behind its high golden walls, the gardens of San Anton Palace are an oasis of colour and calm. A myriad of tree lined walkways lead the way past fountains that play into green tinted ponds. Palm trees, and vast flowering shrubs that fill the air with their rich scent, provide shade. And there are birds; every kind from sparrows to ornamental ducks, black swans and peacocks. But that's in the day time, when we visit the gardens to escape the heat. Everything looks different at night, and the lanterns that guide us produce dark shadows that lurk around every corner. I am glad when at last we arrive at the palace, which is floodlit, and its wide stone steps, pillared terraces and ornate walls are the perfect backdrop for an outdoor night time production of Twelfth Night. We sit on tiered seats to watch the play, and the cicadas, the spotlights, the shadows and the soft night air help Shakespeare come alive, and I am transfixed.

Me at the Malta horse

Mark and Father fishing

I, and later my mother, began to take riding lessons on the Army polo ponies stabled at the Marsa Club, which was a vast outdoor sports and social area for the British Forces, boasting playing fields and tennis courts, stables, indoor and outdoor equestrian arenas and a polo ground. Circumnavigating the complex was a horse racing circuit and, in the centre, the Marsa Clubhouse was set amongst shrubs and lawns kept verdant all year round by a network of sprinkler systems.

We were taught to ride by an awesome, no nonsense horsewoman called Paddy, who introduced us to dressage. Early on, she allocated me a specific pony called Kiki, with whom I was to make a bond and, with Paddy's expert teaching, eventually won a dressage cup at the yearly Malta horse show, something of which I was very proud. But this was not before three years of hard work!

When applied to polo ponies, the word pony is a misnomer! Polo ponies are only called ponies on account of their agility rather than their size. They are large horses, super fit and accustomed to being ridden hard on the Polo ground, and they were not always easy to handle.

This was put to the test every time Paddy decided that we were to have that days' riding lesson in the outdoor arenas. These were in the middle of the sports ground, which meant that we had first to cross the race track to get to them, the stables and indoor arena being on the outside edge of the club grounds. Somehow the ponies always knew when this was going to happen and they would begin to prance before we even left the stable yard.

"Shorten your reins and kick your ponies on,'" Paddy would shout as we approached the racetrack crossing.

The ponies' ears would flick back to clock her voice and you would feel them gather themselves.

"Bring their heads round," Paddy always yelled as inevitably they all took off along the race track. But these ponies had hard mouths and we weren't that strong. I learnt early on to just sit down and give Kiki his head, as trying to stop him too soon by bringing his head round was futile.

I have to admit that I've never been that brave on horseback when it comes to fast gallops. Thrilling though it is I never felt in control of the situation! I grew instead to love dressage, that unison between horse and rider a seemingly miraculous combination.

I wake in the morning as the sun filters through my thin curtains. The heat of the sun on the walls outside gives off the peppery smell of old stone and this seeps in to my bedroom through the open door to the balcony. I stretch and take in the sounds.

The chatter of the budgerigars in their turret aviary is an overriding constant and I love to hear them. I have taken them to heart and spend much of my time watching their antics and learning what they need. They are most entertaining. The accompanying cheeping from the large flock of resident sparrows also echoes around the courtyards below as they pick up spilt seed from under the aviary before flying back into the orangery. Here, they will chase each other between the trees and take long baths in the fountain before the heat builds up.

I hear the cockerel in the farm behind the house repeatedly announcing his presence, and the loud clucking of the laying hens. The farm dog is barking as usual from the roof of the farmhouse. This was disturbing at first but we've become used to it. If we know he has water we try not to worry any more and the sound becomes generic to the day.

The sound of hooves and rumbling wheels gathers as an early morning trotting pony speeds past our gates, the fading sounds then replaced by the distant repetitive call of the man selling diesel from his horse drawn cart in the town, 'Petroleum, Petroleum'.

And from the disused military airfield opposite our house, where Father teaches me to drive when there's no one around, I can already hear the high whine of the model planes as the weekend aviation enthusiasts launch them into the clear blue sky. This reminds me it's Saturday and we are off for the day on 'Call Boy'. I hear Mother in the kitchen assembling the picnic and I leap up to join her.

Mother's picnics were always something to look forward to and she would prepare much of it the day before. She might have made Tabbouleh or chilled Stuffed Vine Leaves. Or she might have prepared a Stuffed French Loaf by cutting a day old baguette in half lengthwise, carefully scooping out the bread from inside, and mixing the breadcrumbs with finely chopped peppers, tomatoes, onions, celery and mint, olive oil, olives and seasoning. She would then pack the stuffing back into the two halves of the loaf, put them together and wrap them firmly in foil overnight and for transportation and then cut into thick slices to serve.

Or she may have made a Hungarian dip she called Liptauer Cheese, by mixing cream cheese with generous amounts of chopped onion, chives, herbs, ground caraway seeds, capers, paprika and seasoning. The mixture was then stored in an airtight container overnight before serving with fresh bread at the picnic.

Whatever picnic Mother had prepared, we always left home a little early to call in at the pastry shop to buy Pastizzi to add to our picnic. These delicious little Maltese pastries, filled with ricotta cheese, were still hot when we bought them and their grease and smell would seep through the brown paper bags to make our mouths water.

Call Boy was the Army launch available for us to use at leisure, which we did with regularity throughout every summer. The vessel had a full crew on board and all we had to do was turn up at the quay, load on our picnic and our friends and cruise along the coast of Malta before dropping anchor off one of the smaller islands of Comino or Gozo. We would spend the day swimming and snorkelling in the crystal clear waters, then motor back as the sun was setting, the adults happily tipsy and we kids tired, sunburned and salty. Those were wonderful days.

Call Boy

I believe I felt as much in my element in the water as I did on dry land in those days. When not diving off Call Boy to swim in offshore waters, we had umpteen favourite places around the island from where we swam and could cool off by the sea. Our quick go-to place was Robb Lido, a vast expanse of flat rocks designated as a private swimming area for forces' families segregated into separate 'officers' and 'other ranks' sections.

Metal steps led straight into the deep water of the bay where large raffia covered rafts were moored at just the right distance away to make a good swimming destination. Many of my school friends based themselves in the 'other ranks' section, which had diving boards and was altogether more fun, and as I got older I spent equal times in both areas. And we were fearless; playing water games, learning to dive from the highest board and free diving from the rafts down to the bottom of the sea to watch the octopi scuttle away under the rocks. Sometimes, as it grew dark, we swam to meet the lights dancing on the water from the other side of the bay where the Dragonara Palace glittered. Sea swimming in the dark is a strange out of body experience that I don't think I've repeated since.

I don't actually remember many sandy beaches, although I believe Malta has developed some since the 1960s! We usually swam off rocks where the sea was clearer, although it was often quite rough and I have scars on my legs to this day from trying to scramble out of the sea in a swell. Father would always be egging me on. He had little patience with fear!

We have swum out to the high rock in the middle of the bay. Father is encouraging us all to climb to the top and his confidence is inspiring. The rock face is sheer and the going hard, but there is a chain hanging down the side that helps us climb up. We arrive at the top in triumph and feel impossibly high up, the sea below us so clear that we can see down to the rocks at the bottom.

Incredibly, one by one, everyone jumps off and eventually I'm on my own. I'm terrified and feel totally unable to move! Father calls up to me from below, offering words of advice and help, first cajoling then resorting to angry impatience and finally disregard as he swims back to shore. I sit for what seems a very long time. I can see the distant shapes of my parents and our friends on the shoreline eating their picnic.

I wait. And breathe. And when they finally lose interest, I jump.

Being an island, the sea around Malta featured greatly in daily life. Fish was a staple diet (as was rabbit and many households kept rabbits as well as chickens to eat) and fish markets were plentiful.

The traditional Maltese fishing boats were small open boats made of wood, brightly painted in different colours with an eye on the front to ward off evil. The fishermen would deftly propel their boats around the bays with a single oar, only using the engine when going out to sea to catch fish in the evenings.

As the sun went down and it got cooler, locals at all the seaside villages around the island would gather to sit and talk by the harbour side. The married women all wore black and the men had flat caps and ill-fitting shoes. Sometimes trotting ponies and their drivers would arrive, instigating animated conversation. Having been driven hard all day in the extreme heat, the sweating animals and men would swim together to cool off.

And on the shoreline beyond the harbour walls, octopus fishermen would climb over the rocks, reaching down to grab their prey from their hiding places, turning them inside out to kill them, then hanging them from their belts in rows, the octopuses tentacles still waving slowly. It was a cruel death for these intelligent creatures and very disturbing to watch.

Our parents' social life was probably the fullest it had ever been. They went out a lot in the evenings and I was either left on my own in the house with the dog or, if Mark was home, the two of us had each other for company.

At bedtime, we always left a note on our parent's bed for them to find when they came home and Mother kept them all. Re-reading them now provides an extraordinary glimpse back to the minutiae of everyday life beyond memory! They also emphasise what a huge role Robinson played in our lives. There was no doubt that she filled the gap of a third child in our mother's life, and her importance and value transferred itself to us all. We all adored her. Our bedtime notes were filled with little descriptions of Robinson's games and antics during the evening, what she had eaten and how she'd been. We knew Mother would want to know and our telling it was acknowledgement that all was well in our world.

Spring picnic

Dodging waves

We had a maid called Madeleine, who came up from Mosta to help in the house. She was very large and moved slowly, although she was an incredibly hard worker, unphased by the heat or the size of the house. She was also a fantastic source of local goings on and kept us informed of all the upcoming Festas, Saint's days and general events in the area. And when Mother and Father gave one of their many large parties, Madeleine proved herself to be invaluable.

For formal dinners, the large mahogany table in the dining room would be laid up with the 'family silver' that came around the world with us! With the silver cutlery and candelabra, Maltese lace napkins and the cut glasses sparkling and reflecting the candles, it always looked so lovely. And I believe Mother earned herself quite a name for being the superb cook she was.

She might have made a large tureen of Hungarian goulash with rice. Or a curry, with side dishes of chopped fruits and nuts, chutneys and Poppadoms. And maybe for pudding, a huge puffy fruit filled Pavlova with a heavily laden cheese board to follow.

As guests arrived Father served drinks, although Paul was often on hand to help with this manly task, and Madeleine and I would help to serve canapes. There would be sherry or spirits on arrival, wine with the meal, port or brandy afterwards. And always cigars on offer!

They once had the idea of dotting small round tables about the dining and sitting room, each one sitting four or six people. The rooms were so big that this idea worked well, although it looked a bit like a restaurant in the end and Mother said people didn't mix so well.

Sometimes, Mother would keep the meal simple and make dozens of large pizzas. The dough would be kneaded and left to rise, then divided, rolled out to fill roasting trays, covered with a rich tomato sauce, topped with anchovies, herbs and cheese, and baked. Madeleine, Mother and I perfected the art of a pizza production line and Paul would carry them upstairs where they would be served with a salad and red wine.

And every party would end up on the roof, under the inky black sky dotted with stars, with Mosta Dome illuminated on one side and Medina in the distance on the other. It was a glorious setting for a party.

As a Strauss Waltz plays loudly out of the Grundig Record Player, Father takes me in his arms and together we dance, the breezes from the open windows cooling us off as we twirl around and around the sitting room, over the black and white tiled floor, until I'm quite dizzy.

"The trouble with your father's dancing," my mother quips, as I grab onto the back of the sofa, laughing triumphantly, "is that he always leads with the same leg and never changes direction!"

But she and Father are laughing with me. I'd finally perfected the Waltz and that was all that mattered!

On the 21 September 1964, Malta was granted her Independence from Britain, an occasion instigating much celebration. After World War Two, following their loyalty and brave resistance, Britain had granted Malta self-government. But during the interim years, a strong pro-Independence movement had developed and a growing anti-British sentiment. I remember the Maltese as being very friendly to us, but I was of course too young to be aware of any political cadence.

There was one event that shook me at the time however. I had just got onto the school bus which was waiting in Mosta to pull out into the road. I sat down in the window seat on the road side and a school bus full of Maltese children overtook us. A boy of about my own age leant out of the open window and spat, aiming at my face. My window was shut luckily, but the globule of slime sliding down the glass and the look of contempt in the boy's face was something I've never forgotten. I didn't think to question it at the time.

I have little memory of the Independence ceremony other than being present at a very grand parade, the Union Jack being lowered and the Maltese Flag hoisted. The Duke of Edinburgh was there, which was an excitement. The previous day, Mother and I had stood by the gates of the governor's residence, where Prince Philip was staying, in order to watch him leave. I had prepared a small posy of flowers that I had hoped to give him. The open car drove out slowly, with Prince Philip sitting in the back waving as crowds of people around us jostled to see him. He didn't stop however, so as he passed us I threw the flowers into his lap. I remember how he jumped! He had the grace to turn around and smile but I've always felt rather bad about that.

We had many visitors from England during our three years in Malta. Our Grandad and Granny Betty came to stay; Father's sister, Joan; our Grandma and Mother's older sister, Joan; and Billie, who came and stayed, living with us for about a year I think.

She took a job in Valletta and had a liaison with a Maltese man who became the butt of many a joke between Mark and me on account of his very proper manners. But it didn't work out and she then left to return to England with 'nervous troubles'. Joan too was suffering from depression. Mother was happy to see her gradually smile and laugh again during her visit, although her growing dependence on alcohol, and later those of Billie's, were a ceaseless cause of anguish for Mother over the coming years.

With Grandma on the beach

Joan's visit

Mother and Billie

Me and Mark

Mother with Robinson at Rob Lido

Our posting in Malta drew to a close. I had done a huge amount of growing up during the three years we were there and there is no doubt that our time on the island proved to be a great influence on me. Inevitably, many of the events I remember are small and of little consequence to any but my younger self. But they remain a memory nevertheless, and this is one.

Our parents have a vet friend who has a tame hawk of some kind. The bird sits on a leather glove on his arm as he climbs the stairs to our roof. There are a lot of stairs but the bird is still, until we reach the top when he tilts his head to hear. We watch as the vet removes the hood from the bird's head and, after a pause, launches him into the sky. We all hold our breath. There seems to be a very real chance that the bird will not return or will be shot at. But the bird doesn't know this and soars high into the sky, calling. He wheels around a few times, then suddenly dives towards us and lands gracefully on the vet's arm and gets given a piece of meat. He does this a few times and it's beautiful to watch. But we sigh collectively in some relief when he is finally hooded once again for his trip home. He wasn't aware of the danger of course, but I still wonder if those few moments of sublime freedom were enough?

Mark, 1966

I had been 'put down' for a school called Bradfield. I had visited this Gothic place and found it desperately academic. In short, the least suitable place for a student such as me would be difficult to find. The Common Entrance pass bar for Bradfield was set at 56%. I achieved 49%. This failure to achieve a required grade was clearly an embarrassment, both for my parents and for the prep school. Not only had the pupil failed but the school had also failed in its promise to prepare the lad to the academic level that it had undertaken to do.

The safety net public school of last resort for such failures was St Bees in what was then Cumberland, now Cumbria. St Bees was founded by one Archbishop Grindal in circa 1750 and evolved into a semi outward-bound type school. I found it to be a particularly inward-bound experience. Once again, very keen on corporal punishment as the chosen route to control but, with the onset of puberty, I found this aspect of the school risible. The very fact that a man could make me grab a piping hot radiator whilst he stroked his split cane switch and then give me 'six of the best', made me laugh over the pain.

St Bees was the only public school I knew of that required short trousers to be worn by pupils up until the age of eighteen, and I found it perverse and verging on the limits of decency. In any event, my attitude to 'authority' was further strengthened as being cruel, asinine and pointless. I now believe that my modus operando was guided as much by an inherent laziness as a philosophical pose. I wanted to do as little as possible. Just enough. I neither excelled at nor enjoyed any of my classes or teachers, with the possible exception of English Literature. I hated cross-country runs with a vengeance and was pretty mediocre at rugby and cricket.

St Bees is a village on the North West coast of Cumbria and the village is the school. A pupil's first term was spent in a junior house then on to the 'big' house with all the incumbent rites of passage. My junior house was called Eaglesfield. A typical day started at 5.30am and began with a run with swimming trunks under our shorts to the beach and, regardless of temperature, a swim out beyond the surf line for two hundred and fifty yards then back to the beach. No towels were allowed, so we would run back to the house wet and shivering, our shorts and shirts rolled up and clutched in our right hands. Once back at the house, a group tepid shower, breakfast of porridge, then a further run to Foundation House to the Assembly Hall, then chapel and lessons.

The first term was scary. I knew absolutely no one and developed an aloofness that rather prevented me making friends but was the only way I could find to build a wall around my insecurity and shyness. It took me some time to recognise other boys who thought similarly to me and who had even less respect for authority than I. Jeff Kay, an American, became a good friend and we did produce some covert and overt mayhem together over the years. He used to bring LP's over from Los Angeles, his hometown. Stuff I still listen to today; Love, Tim Buckley, Dylan, Tom Paxton, Hendrix; so many. The war in Vietnam was ticking along nicely by this stage and we were nascent members of all kinds of protest movements. Ironically, a few years later, he was shot dead whilst serving as a soldier in Vietnam aged eighteen.

I moved on to Grindal House, complete with fagging and flogging but with a halfway decent house master, Coates, who clearly didn't much like me but was fair handed and only whipped you when he thought that you'd deserved it. Another popular punishment was having to run either a 'Range Triangle' or a 'Trees Triangle'. Those running these punishment runs could be observed across the valley every step of the way from the prefect's office block. I seemed to spend my life running around these triangles and if one of the prefects thought I 'dawdled' along the way, I was made to repeat it.

On the plus side, I learnt to play the French Horn badly, there were a handful of good teachers and regardless of my academic achievements or dearth of, I did receive a halfway decent education, more by osmosis than concentration, which has stood me in good stead over the years and kept my ears pricked with a degree of sentience to the nuances of our times.

We're up to 1967-ish now and times were surely changing. The only glimpse through the dirty windowpane that we got, locked up in Cumberland with no female company, was through music, books, radio, and endless discussions. Even pre-drugs and long hair and clothes, we or I learnt to differentiate between those who were mindful, 'heads' as we called them, and those who were intolerant of change and wished the status quo to remain. I have the same mind set to this day and am thankful for it. Such apartheid, if you will, gives one a hierarchical view of humanity, not born of colour or creed but of perceived perception which makes one a snob by any other name. It's quite late at the time of writing so this probably sounds as pretentious as it reads.

St Bees ground on. I truly did have the feeling that I was imprisoned with my release date a distant dream. I had one last holiday in Malta after my first term at St Bees, which was as good fun as ever. And as always I spent the first two weeks or so of the school holiday on tenterhooks waiting for my school report to arrive. This was invariably either bad or mediocre, to the disappointment of my parents, and a cloud would descend on me for a few days. There would be sighs of disappointment from both parents and monosyllabic replies to my utterances, but it passed over in time after I resolved to do better the following term. The fact that we went through this charade three times a year could have been black humour in an overacted Oscar Wilde play.

England—July 1966

Philippa

In the summer of 1966, we packed up the Heavy Luggage and prepared to leave the island. We were to be posted to the UK. I was fifteen, Mother was thirty-nine and Father was forty-three. We were all so young but I remember that it felt like an ending as we smiled our way through a farewell party in the waiting area at Luqa Airport, surrounded by so many friends who had become dear to us.

Robinson had been shipped back to England three months in advance in order to begin her six months' quarantine. This was heartbreaking for Mother I'm sure, and I don't think Robinson fared very well in kennels either. She pined and didn't eat for a long time. As soon as we arrived in England, Mother visited the kennels and apparently when Robinson saw her, she appeared to faint! Once she had recovered, their reunion was joyful, but Mother was asked by the kennels not to go again over the following three months as Robinson had pined and refused food all over again.

It's a curious thing but I have absolutely no idea what Father did next! But when we first arrived back in England I guess he was de-briefed and was then given 'leave'. We stayed the rest of the summer in a wonderful rambling country house in Surrey called Ranmoor, generously lent to us by a friend of Father's, Major General Johnny Frost. Mark arrived for the holidays and we spent the summer there visiting and entertaining friends and relations and enjoying Ranmoor's luxurious accommodation. The gardens boasted a tennis court, swimming pool and croquet lawn, and we made full use of them all.

Our father's first cousin, Anne, lived not far away and she, her husband and their three daughters came to visit us a few times. This began a close association with Anne and the family that continued for many years. The girls were younger than me but went to Tormead School for Girls in Guildford and, on Anne's recommendation, it was decided that I too would join the Fifth Form at Tormead that September in time for my GCE's the following year.

We were given an Army quarter just outside the village of Mytchett in Surrey, 25 Keogh Close, and this was our home for the next eighteen months. What Father's actual job was at the adjacent Keogh Barracks or in Aldershot I don't think I ever knew, and I guess I never asked! He was just collected in an Army staff car by a driver every morning to go to 'work'!

Our house was nice enough, in a row of identical others, but with a reasonably large garden that backed onto the type of pine forest so typical of Surrey. There were excellent walks to be had in the forest and Mother and Father bought me a Siamese cat I named Sheba who came for walks with us on a lead as we slowly got to know the smells and sounds of the English countryside. Over that first winter we were woken many times at night by the sound of a vixen calling and Mother and I would meet on the landing, wide-eyed and rather scared. We had no idea what it was. We had a lot to learn about British wildlife!

I had what I considered the best room in the house as it had a very small study attached. I had my books and treasures in there, maps on the wall and my art projects spread around, and it was here that I spent the following summer swatting for my GCE's. But before that school! And I hated every minute.

I would get the train from Ash Vale to Guildford station from where it was only a short walk up to the school. Initially welcomed as a novelty into the group of 'trendy' girls who had been together since nursery school, I was eventually resented or disliked and was subjected to the sort of psychological bullying by the same group that only girls are so good at. Ultimately, there were others who became good friends, but that first year was hard, and not made any easier by the school itself.

Tormead at that time was a bastion of rules, implemented by a strict headmistress who based her regime on a mode of conduct rapidly becoming outdated, such as requiring teenage girls to kneel on the floor of the hall every morning so that staff could check that skirts touched the floor, sometimes also to prove that the uniform thick navy blue underpants were being worn! But this was the early days of the miniskirt and social rebellion, and we flouted the clothes rule wherever we could. Our pleated school skirts were rolled up around our waists and our hats stuffed into school satchels the minute we were outside the school gates! I believe some things never change and the same is being done today!

My education continued however, still poor at French, Maths and Sciences, I nevertheless redeemed myself at English, Art, Geography and History. This may have been the 1960s but times were not changing that much in the type of education offered to girls who weren't too academic. We had lessons in book-keeping, shorthand and typing, all of which admittedly have seen me in good stead over the years. Also cookery and sewing, both taught to a very high standard it has to said! And as Mother had continued to make our clothes over the years and had instructed me well, I enjoyed perfecting the art of dressmaking. We played netball and hockey in heavy serge knee length culottes that stripped the skin from the inside of our thighs in the winter. We had athletics in the summer and I was able to earn a few good points for my house in the hundred-yard sprint and long jump. I took a diploma in Public Speaking and Bird Recognition, and I read avidly, modern fiction as well as all the classics. But it was art that I loved the most and, from early on, I decided that I wanted to go to art school.

We went up to St Bees once to visit Mark for an exeat weekend. It was a long drive and St Bees was bleak. Once we arrived, however, I wasn't allowed out of the car on account of being a girl who might distract the boys! So I sat in the car whilst Mother and Father collected Mark and we stayed in a rather grim Bed and Breakfast.

When Mark came home from school for holidays, we had as much family fun as ever. He and I would go for long bike rides together around Mytchett Pond and catch up on each other's news. And as a family we discovered and fell in love with Dartmoor, camping rather disastrously once (we all quarrelled I seem to remember, although about what I don't know!) before staying for two summers running in a rather primitive little cottage that had an outside toilet and no bathroom. Instead, Father would bring his Army canvas campaign bath, put it in a sheltered place in the garden and fill it up with tepid water for us all to take turns.

My GCE results were good enough but I decided to concentrate on art. Tormead was offering a new sixth form initiative that following school year, giving pupils the chance to study for A levels in only one year, and I jumped at the chance. We were newly exempt from wearing uniform in the sixth form and I embraced that last year with more enthusiasm than I had the first. I also took Sociology and Human Biology lessons with the option of sitting a GCE exam in those subjects at the end of the year. I made new friends in the sixth form and we all began to hang out in Guildford in our spare time, have a few boyfriends, go to parties and concerts, and generally do what sixteen and seventeen year olds do. Mother and Father however, proved to be incredibly strict about curfews and being out alone with boys. This resulted in many a breakneck drive back from a party in order to return within the time stated, and then having to endure an awkward farewell in the driveway, where Mother and/or Father would always be on the doorstep waiting with a torch!

At some point Father was sent out to Australia on a mission, I don't know what! But I remember he was away for quite a while. And on his return home he seemed changed, very preoccupied and prone to long silences. Mother eventually learnt that during his time in Australia he had met a woman with whom he'd became close.

I remember the rows mostly, Mother's distress and Father's unresponsive silences, then finally Mother learning that the woman was shortly arriving in England. Father seemed defeated at this point, but Mother wasted no time in driving up to Heathrow with me in tow, where we managed to meet the relevant flight. I'm not sure what she had planned to say, but when we introduced ourselves to the woman in question (she was wearing a bright red suit with a pill box hat), she turned tail and literally ran away!

Perhaps Mother's actions had the intended result however, as life at home returned to some semblance of normality and I presumed that a truce or agreement had finally been made. But in hindsight I know that the relationship Father had with this woman, in whatever form it was at the time, remained an unspoken wedge between them. And much later, when our parents had separated and Father had married her in haste, he grew to rue the day he'd ever met her.

Meanwhile, Father was then posted to Bulford in Wiltshire and went on ahead whilst Mother and I stayed in Keogh Close for me to finish my last term at Tormead and take my exams. Needless to say, I failed to gain a good grade in Sociology and Human Biology GCE's after only a year, although I'd thoroughly enjoyed the courses. And although my Art A level grade was more than sufficient to get me into art school, in the end this was not to be. I found an excuse not to follow that path, although it had been my intention for so long, and I have trouble remembering why. Maybe it came down to lack of courage. I don't think I could envisage living away from home at that stage and we were about to move down to Bulford for who knew how long. I was also still very protective of my mother who had not recovered from my father's affair and was increasingly concerned about her sister Joan's mental health. She had trouble sleeping and didn't eat enough and I worried about her. So I shelved the decision of my career until after the summer.

The Army quarter we'd been allocated in Bulford was spacious and very pleasant, although we weren't there for long. I took a holiday job as a waitress in Salisbury, and at the same time had a full and fun filled summer, having met up with a good friend from Malta days whose father had also been posted close by. And at a party in Amesbury in September 1968, aged seventeen and three-quarters, I met Stuart, whose maturity encouraged my parents to loosen their curfew rules somewhat so we could enjoy travelling further afield to parties and clubs in London where Stuart came from.

By this time I had still not made any firm decision as to what to do with the rest of my life. Throughout the summer my parents had been suggesting different career choices. There had been talk about me becoming a nurse, and initially I agreed to the idea. I was offered a place at St Thomas's in London and even went up to be measured for my uniform, before deciding to reject the offer. I had always wanted to work with animals and did a trial few weeks shadowing a veterinary nurse at a practice near by. But that too hadn't felt right. Poor Mother was desperate I think! But she didn't push me.

At the same time, in what must have been a hugely momentous period for my parents, Father left the Army and there was much talk about what he was going to do next. Mother and Father considered running a small guesthouse or hotel and over that summer we all looked around a few properties in Dartmoor, one of those crossroads in life where things might have ended up so differently had they pursued this plan. But in the end, most likely reluctant to forgo his connections with the Arab world, Father took a job with a company called DryClad that sold protective covers for army vehicles in the Middle East. With his ability to speak Arabic and his connections in the area, he was the right man for the job, despite the fact that he was going to need to travel a great deal.

We moved to Kent, initially renting a property in Sittingbourne where I briefly attended a secretarial college (about which I remember nothing) before our parents bought and renovated an enchanting house with a large rambling garden in Canterbury called Hackington Haven. And it was there, in the spring of 1969, that Stuart and I got engaged. Father was working away at the time so we chose to keep it a secret from all but Mother until Stuart could properly ask Father for my hand in marriage!

In the summer of that year, Mark left school and Mother and Father bought him a King Charles Spaniel who completed our menagerie. And in September 1969, Mark and I were enrolled in Canterbury College. Mark was to do his A levels prior to joining the Merchant Navy and I'd somehow got a place on a Post Grad PA course.

Mark embraced his newfound freedom from boarding school by immersing himself wholeheartedly in the vibrant hippy community of Canterbury and all that entailed. With little regard for parental rules or concerns, he began to party hard at night, sleep much of the day and keep poor hours at college. There were nights when he didn't return home at all and Mother would be desperate with worry, sending me to look for him amongst prone bodies asleep on the floors of a variety of party venues thick with the sweet scent of cannabis.

Whilst Father was repulsed by the whole hippy culture, our mother went out of her way not only to understand it for Mark's sake, but to embrace much of the ideology of the times herself, such as women's liberation and equal rights for animals as well as humans. We had a large chalet in the garden of Hackington Haven we called the 'hut'. This we furnished with drapes and cushions and Mother would sit cross-legged on the floor with Mark and his friends discussing the philosophical and existential issues they were all passionate about. Mother would have been in her element admittedly, but there was no doubt that her involvement and their close relationship ultimately saved Mark from losing any sort of life plan.

During the late summer of 1969, Mark fell deeply in love, but it was a relationship that ended with heartbreak. In the spring of 1970 his girlfriend, Susan, became pregnant. And after she'd given birth to their daughter in a home for unmarried mothers she, like thousands of other girls and young women at the time, was left feeling she had no choice but to hand the baby over for adoption. She was expected not to tell a soul, not even her siblings. Unable to see a way past the trauma, she suffered a breakdown and sadly couldn't visualise a way forward with Mark. She later travelled to India with friends and died eighteen months later under mysterious and tragic circumstances.

Mark was deeply affected and distressed by the whole affair, something I believe coloured many of his future relationships. Ultimately, his daughter found him once she reached eighteen, and not only did they grow very close but she became a much loved member of our family. But at the time, it was a wake-up call.

With our mother's support and encouragement, he acknowledged that he was not going to get the exam results in Canterbury that he needed to join the Merchant Navy and he agreed to study for a year at a 'Crammer' in Hastings, where he subsequently passed the relevant exams with flying colours. He was then accepted as an officer cadet in the Merchant Navy, eventually sailing out of Liverpool on the Merchant Vessel Onitsha as a midshipman on a voyage that proved to be the first of his many adventures at sea, both in the Navy and later as a yachtsman sailing the world. And with his innate ability and serendipity to attract a plethora of fascinating people and extraordinary events into his life, Mark amassed many a story to tell.

In the meantime, after finishing college, I took a secretarial job at Pfizers in Sandwich until July 1970 when Stuart and I were married in the little local church of St Stephens, Canterbury.

Sadly, after many years of mental health issues and alcohol dependency, Mother's sister, Joan, had ended her life shortly before our wedding. But Joan's family, my grandma, mother and Billie all put their considerable grief to one side for the wedding, for which I will always feel very humbled and grateful. And following our marriage and honeymoon in Scotland, Stuart and I moved to live in Hampshire where Stuart worked.

Cadet officer 1971

Engagement photo 1968

Family, Canterbury 1968

Once Mark and I had left home, Father continued to travel, very involved with his work and the ex-pat community in the Middle East, all of which he kept very separate from his life with Mother in England. She meanwhile, took a job as an animal photographer and enrolled in a hotel catering course, still hoping that they would pursue their dream. But as time went on, she became increasingly lonely, depressed and resentful of Father's other life, and their marriage didn't survive many more years. A well-planned visit to Hackington Haven by the man Mother had met on board the Asturius all those years previously, and who was ultimately to become her second husband, gave her what she hoped was a ticket for a different life. The house got sold and Mother and Father went their separate ways.

My father once told me he believed that I, as my mother's confidante, could have done more to stop her leaving. This hurt needless to say. Mother had presented her decision to me as the only available solution and I went along with it. She was very eloquent and convinced me of her reasons and I wanted her to be happy. I had two children by then and my life was with them. But in hindsight, all these years later, perhaps if Father had been more able to talk to me about his feelings as Mother had always done, and perhaps if I'd been able to read the letter he wrote to Mother at that time begging her to stay, I wonder if I would have done more to try and stop her going? But she was very unhappy and I'm still not sure Father was prepared to give up his life in the Middle East. In any event, they didn't really give each other time. Mother left and Father, possibly from pride, acted too quickly to fill the gap. And within a very short time, their subsequent relationships, built on past infatuations, proved difficult and destructive. By then it was too late however, and they had many years to acknowledge that they had each made a huge mistake.

Too much time has passed since then for me to know or remember the finer details. That is our parent's story after all and the way it was. But throughout their many life changes and challenges, throughout Mark's and my adulthood, whilst their grandchildren and great grandchildren grew up, and until they both grew old, the love and deep friendship our parents had for each other remained a constant. They kept in contact with one another, helped each other and were often able to spend time together. We continued to be a mini tribe that just got bigger.

Mark, 2017

It is now 2am on the morning of my sixty-fourth birthday. Not old my sister tells me. She also says that 'today is the youngest I will ever be' and other such trite but no less true utterances.

A part of me is amazed that I remain among the living after all this water under the bridge as I've hardly put being kind to my body as a priority, in part for reasons that I'll recount another time, a literary stroll through one's own life, though there are bits that I am not so proud of that I am likely to leave out so as to present myself in a better light!

And so to bed.

Postscript

Philippa

In writing this account, we inevitably had to tackle some childhood issues, and for Mark especially I hope this was in some way cathartic. I wanted to write about a childhood that was unique in many ways, but also very much of its time; about our parents and their unusual relationship; about our exceptional closeness as a family unit and the events that led to its breaking apart; and most especially about the love we shared and the fun we had as we travelled around the world 'following the drum' in the last days of British colonialism!

Despite the drawbacks of their new relationships, our parents went on to lead long and interesting lives. They both travelled extensively with and without their new partners. Mother became an accomplished sculptor and studied counselling and creative writing; Father worked and lived abroad for many years before being widowed, after which he married his cousin, Anne, whose own marriage had broken up many years previously. It was a marriage of convenience for them both I have no doubt, but also one based on a great friendship, and Anne looked after our father until his death, for which Mark and I are forever indebted.

Stuart and I have also done our share of travelling, lived in many houses, shared our homes with many animals and fulfilled many ambitions. And our three grown-up children have a zest for life and adventure that they, in turn, are passing on to their own children.

Mark lived his life in the fast lane where his mercurial intelligence, quirky sense of humour and thought-provoking non-conformist opinions meant he was always stimulating to be around. He had another daughter and he remained close to both his girls. But he died too young, aged sixty-six, on 22 July 2019, before this account of our childhood was completed and long before he went on to write about his remarkable adult life as he had intended.

This is for him.